Collector's Encyclopedia

Of

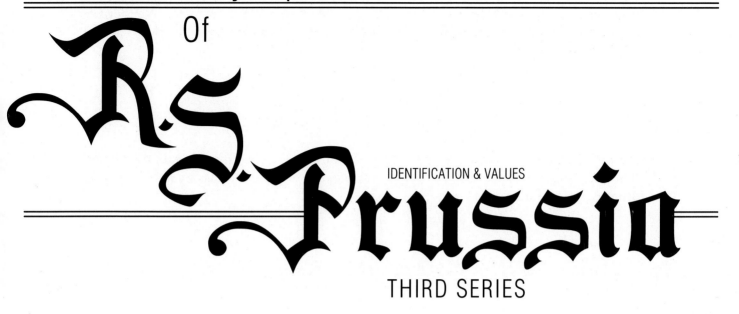

R.S. Prussia

IDENTIFICATION & VALUES

THIRD SERIES

Mary Frank Gaston

COLLECTOR BOOKS

A Division of Schroeder Publishing Co., Inc.

Searching for a Publisher?

We are always looking for knowledgeable people considered to be experts within their fields. If you feel that there is a real need for a book on your collectible subject and have a large comprehensive collection, contact us.

COLLECTOR BOOKS
P.O. Box 3009
Paducah, Kentucky 42002-3009

Top right: Cracker Jar, 5" h x 9" w, $350.00 - 400.00. Middle right: Coffee Pot, 10½" h, $1400.00 - 1600.00. Bottom right: Celery Dish, 12" l x 6" w, $325.00 - 375.00. Top left: Teapot, 3½" h, $500.00 - 600.00. Bottom left: Vase, 9" h, $500.00 - 600.00.

Cover design: Beth Summers
Book design: Pamela Shumaker

Additional copies of this book may be ordered from:

Collector Books
P.O. Box 3009
Paducah, KY 42002-3009
or
Mary Frank Gaston
P.O. Box 342
Bryan, TX 77806

@$24.95 Add $2.00 for postage and handling.

Copyright: Mary Frank Gaston, 1994

Printed by IMAGE GRAPHICS, INC., Paducah, Kentucky

Contents

Acknowledgments

Many individuals deserve acknowledgment for their contribution to this Third Series on R.S. Prussia. Because of the wealth of material, a Fourth Series will follow soon. These editions could not have been completed without the help of each and every one. I am especially grateful to my publisher, Bill Schroeder, Collector Books. He persuaded me to write my first book on R.S. Prussia. I appreciate his encouragement to study and write about this extraordinary china. That book led me to write on other topics as well as a Second Series, and now a Third and a Fourth on R.S. Prussia.

I thank my editor, Lisa C. Stroup, and her staff who have accomplished exceptional work on the production of this new edition. Lisa became editor during the time when my revised edition on Limoges Porcelain was in press. It has been a pleasure to work with her.

I thank my husband, Jerry, who continues to provide support and help for all of my projects. He photographed a number of pieces for this book. He appreciates beautiful porcelain as much as I do, which certainly makes my work much more enjoyable.

I thank all of the many collectors who have asked me to continue my work on Schlegelmilch porcelain. Over the years they have written to me whenever they found anything of interest on the subject. Through their interest, this Third Series became a reality. A large number of them photographed examples from their collections and provided the necessary information about each piece so that more examples of Schlegelmilch porcelain could be shared with a wider audience through this book. A list of these contributors precedes the Dedication. I sincerely appreciate their help.

Special thanks goes to David Mullins, Columbus, Ohio. He has corresponded with me for many years. He is a member of the Ohio Club, and he photographed collections of some of the members so that they could be part of this Third Series. His enjoyment of R.S. Prussia is quite evident in the meticulous care he takes to make such fine pictures and supply detailed information about each piece.

I thank Mr. Mike Edgar for his help in supplying some popular names for certain R.S. Prussia Mold Numbers.

I must single out one person who has provided the greatest help for this book. He is Mr. R. H. (Ron) Capers of Fort Meade, Maryland. Mr. Capers was stationed in Germany with the U.S. military when he began writing to me about Schlegelmilch china some years ago. He had developed an interest in the subject through his mother-in-law, Leonette Wittman. She was a collector and asked him about finding R.S. Prussia in Germany. It was his wife, Noreen, however, who actually found their first piece while at a flea market. From that first example the Capers became "addicted." (This is not uncommon among Schlegelmilch collectors!) They scoured many areas of the country and were successful in locating quite a number of pieces. Mr. Capers photographed the items and sent me pictures on a regular basis. At a time when I was uncertain if there would be a Third Series, he was quite optimistic that one should eventually be published.

Mr. Capers was in Germany when the Berlin Wall fell. Shortly therafter, he was able to travel freely to East Germany and to the city of Suhl. There he made contacts and began to find out information about the Schlegelmilch families and factories. A most important discovery was an unpublished manuscript which had been written about the Schlegelmilch Factories by Bernd Hartwich in 1984. Mr. Capers is fluent in German and was able to translate this work. The information in the thesis changes and clarifies some of the history of the Schlegelmilch factories. He generously provided me with a copy of the translation which enabled me to make revisions concerning the companies.

Mr. Capers has made several more visits to the area. On these visits he has met and talked with local people who have helped him by providing information and sources of documents which relate to the factories and families. He has translated these materials and sent them to me to use as references as well. Some of the people who were instrumental in aiding Mr. Capers in his search for information about the companies are named in a separate list following the contributors of photographs. I certainly extend my thanks for their contributions.

In the spring and fall of 1992 Mr. Capers also visited Tillowitz. Mary and Bob McCaslin, Danville, Indiana, accompanied him on that first trip. The McCaslins are dedicated R.S. Prussia collectors and founding members of International R.S. Prussia Collectors, Inc. Mr. Capers and the McCaslins literally uncovered very important information. They found the Schlegelmilch family grave site behind the old Lutheran Church in Tillowitz. The head stones provided important facts concerning the dates of birth and death of some members of the Reinhold Schlegelmilch family. Pictures of these are shown in an appendix. Funds were provided by the International Association of R.S. Prussia, Inc. so that the site might be cleaned and put in good condition. I now speak for all Schelegelmilch collectors in expressing our thanks for that particular deed.

As collectors and students of Schlegelmilch china, we all owe a special debt of gratitude to Mr. Capers for his diligent efforts to find and provide information about the Schlegelmilchs which has not been previously attainable. I sincerely appreciate the wide assortment of materials and translations he has furnished for me to use for writing this Third Series. Mr. Capers also contributed a large number of photographs. The pictures of the Capers' collection were photographed by Mr. Jonathan Maltman. Mr. Maltman, a friend of Mr. Capers, was also in Germany during the same time. Appreciation is extended to him for his work. Thanks, of course, are due to Mrs. Noreen Capers and her mother, Mrs. Leonette Wittman, for sparking Mr. Capers' interest in Schlegelmilch china! I know Mrs. Capers has been a constant help and support.

In additon to materials and translations, I thank Mr. Capers for reading a draft of the manuscript and providing editorial comments and suggestions. His insights and opinions were quite welcome. For the extraordinary help he has provided, it is my great pleasure to dedicate this Third Series to Mr. R. H. (Ron) Capers.

The following individuals assisted Mr. Capers in Germany:

Herr Reiner Wurzler, Director of the Suhl city and county archives

Frau Eleonore Richter, Suhl Hometown Historical Researcher

Frau Christa Anshütz, Suhl City Guide/Travel Leader

Herr Dr. Martin Kummer, Lord Mayor of the City of Suhl

Herr Dr. Gerhard Soppa from Kreis Falkenberg, scholar of Tillowitz and the R.S. Factory

Herr u. Frau Bösling (Werner & Rosi) from Hamburg, collectors

Herr Dr. Dietrich W. Hahlbrock from Hamburg, husband of the late Brigitte (Koch) Hahlbrock, the last Schlegelmilch family owner of the Reinhold Schlegelmilch Porzellanfabrik, Tillowitz, Upper Silesia

Contributors of Photographs for the Third Series:

Martha and Robert R. Allen, Manns Harbor, NC
Charles and Karen Aschenbeck, Houston, TX
Helen Bailey, Kirksville, MO
Lawrence and Judith Bazaar
John Becker, Columbus, OH
John and Bea Bell
Rose Ellen and Walt Beyer, Omaha, NE
Edda Biesterfeld, Bonn, Germany
Merle N. Blanton, Mechanicsburg, OH
Phyllis Boege, Richton Park, IL
Kerry and Christine Bottcher, Bowmanstown, PA
Dale R. Bowser, Brookville, OH
Freda Bradford
Harold and Barbara Bragg, OH
Noreen and R.H. Capers, Fort Meade, MD
Suzan Cartwright
Richard and Florence Chaney, Myrtle Creek, OR
Nancy J. Clifford, WA
Frances and Terry Coy, Louisville, KY
Phillip Crutcher, Moberly, MO
Edna M. Dennie
Mrs. Ralph Dickey, Mt. Vernon, IN
Sharon Dollos, DuQuoin, IL
Lavaine Donovan
Mike Edgar
Patty Erickson
Margie Fowler, Warrenton, MO
Ken and Debra Fuelberth, IL
Gloria and Byman Geyer, Mansfield, TX
Doris and Carl Gibbs, San Antonio, TX
Nancy Glass, Germantown, TN
John and Sharon Gold, Easton, PA
Robert Gollmar, Rochester, WI
Marian E. Gordon, OH
Nash and Jeannie Hayes, Lebanon, KY
Cynthia Helping, West Milton, OH
John and Deanna Hill, Forest City, IA
Claire Hohnstein
Peter Hohnstein and Deb Schark, Robinson, IL
Maurice and Dee Hooks, Lawrenceville, IL
Maurice L. Hooks, WA
David W. Irwin, Jr.

Nancy A. Jensen, WI
Jody's Antiques, Antique World Mall, North Little Rock, AR
Lee Kirkpatrick
Delbert Krug, Solon, IA
John Law, Fort Dodge, IA
Carl and Phyllis Leohr
Paul Linden, Bellville, WI
Rich and Priscilla Lindstrom, St. Joseph, IL
Debbie Lobel, Arlington, TX
Dr. and Mrs. Wm. J. Luke, Scottsdale, AR
Mary and Robert McCaslin, Danville, IN
Clarence and Ida Meyer, Fort Scott, KS
Marlene and Gene Miller, IN
David Mullins, Columbus, OH
Hoy and Virginia Mullins, WV
Byron Murray
Robert Pompilio, Garden City, NY
Irene Reeves, Alexandria, IN
Kevin Reiman
Jean Riecker, Northville, MI
The Rileys of Ohio
Dale and Amber Rothrock
Tom Rouch, Pierston, IN
Lucille Rowoldt
Barbara and Shelby Smith, Muncie, IN
Donald South
Mr. and Mrs. Oscar Srp, Dayton, OH
Adam Stein, III, High Point, NC
Arlo Stender, Cumberland, IA
Thomas Surratt
Janelle and Gordon Sweeter
Yvonne L. Titchener
Mr. and Mrs. Gary Thomas, Alexandria, IN
Cheryl and Tim van der Hagen, MN
Judy White, Kalamazoo, MI
Joyce and Jack Williams, Irvine, CA
Bonnie and John Willis, El Dorado Hills, CA
Frank Wine, Jr., Portsmouth, VA
Pam Wolfe
Woody Auctions, Douglass, KA
Pete and Viola Zwern, Denver, CO

Other Books by Mary Frank Gaston

**Dedicated to
Mr. R. H. (Ron) Capers**

Preface

The study of Schlegelmilch china has been actively pursued by thousands of dedicated collectors for over twenty five years. At some point during the late 1960's, china marked with the distinctive green wreath, red star, and "R.S. Prussia" began to be widely collected across the United States and in Canada as well. Examples were rather plentiful, and the china was distinguished by several characteristics which made it easy to recognize. The china was not only very fine quality and delicately thin, but it was also molded into elaborate and intricate shapes, highlighted by unique decorations. Transfer designs of a number of subjects such as beautiful women of a by-gone era, quaint pastoral and village scenes, exotic birds, rare animals, and vivid floral designs were enhanced by striking finishes and background colors. Pieces were bordered and accented with gold. The china fulfilled all requirements for inherent collectibility.

Concrete information about the factory which manufactured the china, however, remained scant as collectors began to search for the history about the company. The word "Prussia" in the mark indicated that the china had been made in an area of Germany prior to World War I. After the war Prussia ceased to exist as a state. That particular area of Germany had been shuttered from the West by the "iron curtain" after World War II. Consequently, knowledge about the factory which produced the china was difficult to obtain. Reference books about china production prior to World War II were not helpful, because the china was really not old enough to have been considered "antique" before that time. Information was largely found through old catalog advertisements which showed examples and sometimes the mark.

An American, Clifford Schlegelmilch, wrote a book in 1970 entitled *My Ancestors China*. He illustrated the book with many examples and wrote a brief history of the factories which produced the china. His information was gathered from some family members and at least one old employee of the factory (Schlegelmilch, 1970:14). Numerous marks were shown in the book which were noted to have been used by three different Schlegelmilch factories: the Erdmann Schlegelmilch Company; the R.S. Schlegelmilch Company; and the Oscar Schlegelmilch Company. This publication was really the first informative one about Schlegelmilch china. As a result, the material it contained became the basis of knowledge, not only for collectors, but also for

other writers about china and ceramic marks. German as well as American authors used Schlegelmilch's book as a primary reference source for the Schlegelmilch factories and the marks they used.

During the same year that Clifford Schlegelmilch's work was published, a pamphlet, *Why R.S. Prussia*, was self-published by C. Chumley Hayden. Two other self-published books eventually followed: *The Treasures of R.S. Prussia*, 1978, by Eileen Barlock, and *My Collection*, 1979, by Don Sorenson. George Terrell's *R.S. Prussia*, was published by Books Americana in 1980. My first book on the subject, *The Collector's Encyclopedia of R.S. Prussia*, was published by Collector Books also in 1980. It was followed in 1986 by my *Second Series*.

In my first book I presented my own chronology of marks based on examples, decoration, and available historical information to establish a period of time for when each of the various marks might have been used. This had not been attempted by other writers on the topic. Robert E. Röntgen's book on German ceramic marks was released in 1980. A number of Schlegelmilch marks were shown, and some were also dated. In my Second Series I compared my chronology of marks against Röntgen's time periods and gave my arguments for either agreeing or disagreeing with his dates.

In 1990 the "iron curtain" fell, and almost overnight it seems, the Cold War began to wind down and finally was ended. It became possible to travel and communicate more easily with countries in Eastern Europe. Through the efforts of one very dedicated collector, R. H. Capers, new information about the Schlegelmilch factories was discovered. Mr. Capers was able to locate an unpublished thesis which was entitled *The History of the Suhl Porcelain Factories*, 1861-1937. This paper was written by Bernd Hartwich as a Technical School final term paper in 1984. Mr. Capers obtained an original copy from the city and county archives in Suhl. He was able to make a full translation of the document and generously provided me with a copy.

The information in this manuscript does indeed shed light on the history of the factories. It includes some basic facts which are contrary to some of those originally stated in Clifford Schlegelmilch's book. I would like to emphasize that I do not mean to indicate that Mr. Schlegelmilch knowingly presented erroneous information concerning the Schlegelmilch factories. He was working with all of the information sources he was able to find. While he was conducting his research, freedom of information from the sites of the factories was not possible.

Because of the availability of this new reference source, however, it is now necessary to correct some of the information regarding the Schlegelmilch ceramic factories. In this edition I have drawn from that document, as well as from some other German materials which were also discovered and translated by Mr. Capers. I have not presented the paper in its entirety. Rather, I have tried to show the relevant historical dates and other pertinent matter relating to the factories' history and production which was detailed in the manuscript and the other new reference sources.*

In addition to the manuscript, Mr. Capers and Mary and Bob McCaslin also made another important discovery regarding the Reinhold Schlegelmilch family. They visited Tillowitz in the spring of 1992. They found the family grave plot at a cemetery behind the old Lutheran church. The site had been neglected for a very long time, but by taking the time to carefully search the grounds, they were rewarded. A marker for the "Schlegelmilch Family" was found as well as the head stones for several family members. This was a very important find because the birth and death dates were inscribed on the stones. Those dates help to unravel some of the family history which remained unclear even in the manuscript written by Hartwich.

This Third Series discusses the revised historical information about the companies and includes a revised chronology for the major R.S. marks used by the Rein-hold Schlegelmilch factories. The photographs in this Third Series are devoted to the china which carries the R.S.P. Wreath and Star Mark, or the RSP mark combined with another mark (such as "Royal Hamburg"), or the Wheelock Prussia mark. Other "R.S." marks used by the Reinhold Schlegelmilch factories such as "R.S. Suhl," "R.S. Steeple," "R.S. Tillowitz," and "R.S. Poland" will be covered in the forthcoming Fourth Series. Marks and photographs for the Erdmann Schlegelmilch Factory, the Oscar Schlegelmilch Factory, and the Carl Schlegelmilch Factory will also be presented in the Fourth Series.

The Mold Identification System has been maintained and expanded for the R.S. Prussia examples. The Mold Identification Chart can be found in the Appendices. Some of the Molds identified in the First and Second Series have been changed, deleted, or placed under other marks. For example, the Hidden Image Mold will be found under "Ambiguous Marks" and the Iris Variation Mold will be found under "Steeple Marks," in the forthcoming Fourth Series. Because most of the RSP mold changes will be included only in that edition, an index to those changes will be included only in that edition.

A Floral Decoration number has been assigned to many of the floral patterns found on R.S. Prussia china. An Index for these patterns is provided. An Index for Objects and one for R.S. Prussia Decoration Themes is also included. Several Appendices contain information and photographs relating to the Reinhold Schlegelmilch family and factories. A Value Guide is also included.

*The manuscript written by Bernd Hartwich and translated by R. H. Capers is available from the International Association of R.S. Prussia Collectors, Inc. for a small fee to cover copying and mailing costs. Contact Mary McCaslin, 22 Cantebury Dr., Danville, IN 46229. Inquires for club membership may be sent to Mrs. Jenny Lou Huston, Secretary, 14215 Turtle Rock, San Antonio, TX 78232.

Revised Historical Origins
of the
Schlegelmilch Porcelain Factories
Suhl and Mäbendorf
Langewiesen
Tillowitz

Suhl and Mäbendorf

Suhl, the town where the Schlegelmilch porcelain factories originated, has an intricate and varied history as part of the Germanic region of Thuringia. The town had been under different rulers from feudal times until, as a result of the Treaty of Vienna enacted on May 22, 1815, it became a part of the region acquired by the German state of Prussia. Hartwich (1984: 2) describes the town after that date as "...a part of the County of Schleusingen, Prussian District of Erfurt, Province of Saxony." It is interesting to note the several names mentioned here: "Suhl," "Thuringia," "Prussia," and "Saxony" are all words which can be found in marks on Schlegelmilch china.

The foundation of Suhl as a center for porcelain production was the result of the town's earlier iron ore industry. That business was described as being at its peak during the sixteenth century. It led, in fact, to the development of weapons manufacturing as well in Suhl during that time. Over the next three hundred years the iron ore became depleted, and mining for the mineral had ceased in Suhl by the end of the 1800's. The forges in Suhl needed to be converted to other uses. It was discovered that those forges could be adapted to manufacturing porcelain (Hartwich, 1984: 3).

True porcelain had been made in Germany since about 1708. Historically, the discovery of the technique in the Western world has been attributed to Johann Friedrich Böttger, an alchemist of Meissen. His work led to the founding of the Royal Meissen Porcelain Company. The secret of making true porcelain was guarded for many years. Over time, however, the knowledge was carried to other regions in Germany as well as to other countries through workers going from one area to another. Porcelain factories, other than Meissen, were operating in Germany under Royal patronage during the middle 1700's.

Twelve porcelain factories were established in Thuringia during the early period of the industry's development in Germany from about 1760 until 1800, beginning with the Sitzendorf and Volkstedt factories (Hartwich, 1984: 4). During the 1800's private ownership of porcelain factories became possible. Thus, the way was open for individuals to start their own china factories. It is not surprising that two people in Suhl decided to try their hand at this particular business.

Three porcelain factories under the name of Schlegelmilch were actually put into production after 1860. This occurred about one hundred years after the Sitzendorf and Volkstedt factories were established in Thuringia. According to Hartwich (1984: 6, 19, 27), the Erdmann Schlegelmilch Factory was founded in 1861; the Reinhold Schlegelmilch Factory was founded in 1869; and the Carl Schlegelmilch factory was founded in 1882. While these same dates are really not new information to collectors, the family relationship between the owners of the E.S. and R.S. factories is not what has previously been thought.

The name "Schlegelmilch" is a common Germanic one, especially for the area where the factories were located. While there may have been some connection between Reinhold's and Erdmann's families, the two were not brothers. They did not have a father named "Rudolph," nor was the famous "R.S." trademark symbolic of his name as stated by C. Schlegelmilch (1970: 16). According to a genealogical study of the family which was made by R. H. Capers between 1990 and 1992, Erdmann and Reinhold apparently came from two separate families. The name "Rudolph," in fact, does not appear in any of the historical documents found pertaining to either the Erdmann Schlegelmilch or Reinhold Schlegelmilch families. The Reinhold Schlegelmilch family tree, which resulted from this research, is shown in the Appendices. Erdmann Schlegelmilch's family tree will be in the Fourth Series.

The origins of the three Schlegelmilch porcelain factories in Suhl are discussed in the following sections under separate headings. The information is largely based on the 1984 Hartwich study as translated by R. H. Capers.

The Erdmann Schlegelmilch Factory

Perhaps the most interesting new fact concerning the factories is that the ES factory was not founded by Erdmann Schlegelmilch. It was established by his sons: Leonhard, Carl August, and Friedrich Wilhelm (Hartwich, 1984: 8). Carl August, the oldest son of Erdmann, inherited an iron forge when Erdmann died in 1844. Events of the mid 1800's, such as the lack of iron ore and high mining costs associated with trying to extract the remaining ore, caused forge owners to close their businesses or look for alternative uses for the plants and equipment. The Schlegelmilch brothers "experimentally converted in 1861, under the management of Leonhard Schlegelmilch, a part of their forge for the manufacture of porcelain" (Harwich, 1984: 8). It is necessary to stress the word "experimentally." Evidently, there was not any large scale porcelain production at first. This may explain, in part, why information on dating the various E.S. marks cannot be traced to those years of the early 1860's and 1870's.

The forge could be converted to porcelain production, because it already had gas, glazing, and drying furnaces. The same type of equipment is also necessary for firing china. Leonhard, manager of the factory, is described by Hartwich (1984: 10) as using all means to persuade workers from other porcelain factories in the area to leave their jobs and come to work for him. We are told that Leonhard was trained as a sculptor at the Art Academy in Dusseldorf. Consequently, his first production of porcelain was geared to artistic wares. Because of stiff competition in that line of items from longer established factories, the ES factory turned its production to more utilitarian ware (Hartwich, 1984: 10). The porcelain factory was named for the brothers' father, Erdmann. Once a marking system was implemented, the marks incorporated his initials or even his full name.

The production of the factory was intended for the export trade. The range of items made was quite varied, consisting largely of table china and decorative accessories. The company's efforts evidently met with success, because over the years the iron forge was completely turned over to porcelain manufacturing. The factory exported not only to England and the United States, but it also shipped china to France, Italy, and Russia. The business experienced cyclical ups and downs over the years during the 1870's and 1880's as the economic circumstances of the export countries fluctuated. The raising of tariffs by these countries was the major hardship for the factory.

The management of the ES factory also changed over time. In 1881 Leonhard placed his son Carl, from his first marriage, in charge of the business. In 1882 Julius Martin Schlegelmilch, Leonhard's son from a second marriage, took over the management of the company. In 1885 another son from Leonhard's first marriage, Oscar, joined Julius Martin in becoming partners with their father in the business (Hartwich: 1984: 12).

During the late 1880's the ES factory continued to expand its facilities. Increased tariffs by the United States for imported china effectively closed that source as a market, however. Consequently, on September 1, 1891 the partnership established in 1885 ended, and Julius Schlegelmilch became the only owner of the company. His half brother, Oscar, went to another town, Langewiesen (also in Thuringia), in 1882 and established his own factory. Leonhard died in 1898 at the age of seventy-four (Hartwich, 1984: 13).

Tariffs for imported china into the United States were dramatically reduced in 1894 with the implementation of the Wilson Customs Bill. As a result, the ES factory was able to take advantage of the situation. Business was so good that the plant was expanding once again. The "boom" was short-lived, however, because the McKinley Tariff Bill was enacted in 1896. That bill brought back the higher duties on china imported to the United States. Local conditions in Suhl such as increased freight and coal prices as well as the Japanese entry into the American china market after 1891 were other factors which led to the decline of the company during the late 1890's. Although Julius Schlegelmilch tried to maintain his production, even continuing to expand and remodel his facilities during 1898 and 1899, it was necessary to reorganize the company on December 14, 1899. At that time it was converted to a joint stock company with Julius retaining control through owning the largest number of shares (Hartwich, 1984: 14).

The early years of the twentieth century saw the rise and fall of the company again. The problems were basically the same as in the other years: United States tariffs, Japanese competition, and rising domestic costs for coal and other supplies needed for making china. In 1906 the joint stock company organized in 1899 declared bankruptcy with the result that the company was dissolved on January 31, 1908 (Hartwich, 1984: 15). However, the company was re-registered on February 8, 1908. Attempts were once more initiated to keep the factory in production. Facilities again were expanded and improved. Increased American tariffs coupled with the beginning of World War I caused the company to drastically reduce its production. The lucrative overseas markets were closed to the company, and workers were drafted into the military. The factory was taken over by the Berlin War Office in 1917 (Hartwich, 1984: 16).

After the end of World War I the company was again able to recover and re-enter the export market. The business enjoyed another expansion not only in workers but also in the increased variety of items manufactured. But as with the pre-war years, conditions soon appeared from which the company was finally unable to recover. The problems centered in 1922 on the local high German inflation, causing orders to fall. Obviously, with fewer orders production had to be reduced over the next several years. The work week was limited to four days in 1926, and the work force was cut by one third (Hartwich, 1984: 17). All of these factors resulted in escalated costs for manufacturing. The high costs of coal and raw materials as well as increased tariffs, not only in America, but also in England, combined to create too large an obstacle for the company to overcome. The world wide Depression of the 1930's was the final blow for the business. Hartwich (1984: 17) notes:

> In 1930, 250 workers were still employed, but by October/December 1931, only 116 remained... Starting in January 1931, no more orders came in; therefore, the number of workers decreased further so that in October/December 1933, only 79 workers were still employed... In the Summer of 1935, the Erdmann Schlegelmilch porcelain factory closed down... In the next two years, the factory facilities and buildings were sold. On 10 April

1937, the Erdmann Schlegelmilch Porcelain Factory Open Trading Company was stricken from the Trade Register in Suhl.

Marks and photographs of the Erdmann Schlegelmilch Company will be covered in the Fourth Series.

The Reinhold Schlegelmilch Factory

Hartwich (1984: 19) states that in 1868, Reinhold Schlegelmilch purchased a forge which had been owned by Kaspar Schlegelmilch since 1856. However, no family relationship is mentioned between Reinhold and Kaspar. It is also mentioned that Carl August Schlegelmilch, Erdmann's son, was co-owner of the forge; however, his part was also bought out by Reinhold.

Reinhold purchased the forge for the purpose of establishing a porcelain factory. The name of the enterprise became "Reinhold Schlegelmilch." The company was formally registered in Suhl on October 24, 1869 (Hartwich, 1984: 19). The factory soon became the largest in the area, especially overshadowing the Erdmann Schlegelmilch factory. After ten years Reinhold's factory employed more than twice the number of workers of the ES factory. The production of the two potteries was similar. Chiefly, table wares were manufactured for the export trade.

In the 1870's and early 1880's Reinhold continued to expand his facilities. His company did not suffer from the external tariffs and local economic situations of that period as much as the ES Company. The reason for this, Hartwich (1984: 20) explains, is because Reinhold's interests were diversified. For example, he owned cattle which enabled him to have a means of transportation for his raw materials and finished manufactured goods between Suhl and Grimmenthal, the closest railhead. There was no rail line in Suhl until 1882. Transportation in and out of the local area was thus a major concern prior to that time.

Severe restrictions of the American McKinley Tariff of 1884, however, did affect Reinhold's company. Prices for his china fell, but he continued to hire more workers and enlarge his factory over the next several years. The factory during this time is said to have produced only "staple commodities," because they not only sold well but could also be easily stored (Hartwich, 1984: 20). This would presumably be a source of supply to be sold at a later time when conditions were better.

Hartwich (1984: 20) states that "On 12 October 1886" Reinhold "gave the business procuration to his brother, the merchant, Otto Schlegelmilch, and on 17 December 1887, to his brother, Ehrhard Schlegelmilch." The term "business procuration" is interpreted as meaning that the person so named was brought into the company to actively take part in the business. Note that while Hartwich says "Ehrhard" was Reinhold's brother, research on the family tree indicates that he was Reinhold's son. This makes sense if one looks at the date of

birth for Ehrhard. Reinhold was born in 1837, and Ehrhard was born in 1866. These dates were on the graves found in Tillowitz in 1992. It should be pointed out that Ehrhard may be spelled in several different ways, such as "Erhard," "Erhardt," "Ehrhardt," and "Ehrhard." From this point on the name will be spelled "Erhard."

The Reinhold Schlegelmilch factory in Suhl grew larger and larger from the late 1880's through the 1890's. The 1893 Coburg Ceramic Directory lists show rooms for the company in Amsterdam, Berlin, Bucharest, Constantinople, and Hamburg. It was shown to have had 500 employees. The company built facilities such as housing and shops for its workers, becoming a type of "company town." In 1894 the owners of the factory were registered as Reinhold Schlegelmilch and Arnold Schlegelmilch (Reinhold's son) in Suhl, and Erhard Schlegelmilch in Tillowitz (Hartwich, 1984: 21).

Like the ES Company, the easing of the American duty restrictions of the Wilson Tariff in 1894 made it possible for the RS factory in Suhl to export more china to the United States. This resulted in a few more profitable years for the business. The reprieve did not last long, as higher tariffs were once more imposed with the McKinley Bill of 1896. This, together with the increased Japanese competition for the American market, was very detrimental to the factory. Attempts were made to modernize the facility by introducing electricity as a source of energy. The plant was enlarged again as well. Local conditions also worked against the company, because raw materials for making the china as well as coal had to be brought in from outside the local area. Rail costs for such transportation was very expensive.

Reinhold Schlegelmilch died on February 19, 1906 (Hartwich, 1984: 23). The date of his death is one of interest to collectors, because it is much earlier than suggested by Clifford Schlegelmilch (1970: 34). He mentions that there was correspondence from Reinhold Schlegelmilch to his (Clifford's) mother in January of 1929. A portion of the letterhead with the date is shown on page 14 of his book. A signature of "Reinhold Schlegelmilch" is also shown; seemingly it is from the letter (the letter was not reproduced). It is obvious that Reinhold's date of death and this signature from 1929 are in conflict. The explanation is probably that the company used the name "Reinhold Schlegelmilch" in correspondence after his death, even as a signature, based on the name of the company. This may have been a common practice, because a letter from the Erdmann Schlegelmilch Factory has "Erdmann Schlegelmilch" as a signature. He had died before the factory was even established.

Reinhold's death occurred some years prior to World War I. Production in the factory began slowing down some years after his death. Only 300 workers are listed for the company by the Coburg Ceramic Directory of 1910. The factory was still able to operate on a limited scale during the first years of the war. It suffered the same problems as the ES factory, however, namely lack of orders and lack of workers. The employees were either being drafted or changing jobs by going to work for the weapon manufacturers.

Arnold, as head of the Suhl factory during those years, made a plea to the Board of Trade in Erfurt on September 18, 1915 that he be allowed to keep at least five skilled workers so that the factory could be put in operation again when the War was over. If this did not occur, Arnold stated

> "...I will have to shut down my company completely, would never re-open and would be forced to transfer the entire factory to Tillowitz in Upper Silesia." (Hartwich, 1984: 23)

Arnold's plea was not granted, and thus the Reinhold Schlegelmilch factory in Suhl closed in December 1917. It was then relocated in Tillowitz.

The Carl Schlegelmilch Factory

Very little information is known regarding the third Schlegelmilch china factory which was located in Mäbendorf, a suberb of Suhl. This business was started by Carl Schlegelmilch, Leonhard's son by his first marriage. (Leonhard was Erdmann's son.) Carl became the owner of the Mäbendorf Forge in 1882. Evidently, he left his father's business, the ES factory, to start another china manufacturing outlet in the area. He was the only owner of that company until 1912. At that time, it became an open trade company under the name "Mäbendorf Porcelain Factory, Schlegelmilch & Co." Three people (various ES relations), became partners with Carl. They included Carl's half brother, Julius Martin, who was also in charge of the ES factory. That partnership lasted for less than one year, because records indicate that Carl Schlegelmilch was once again the only owner on May 27, 1913. The business procuration was given to Carl's son, Hans, on

that same day. But Hans was replaced by Carl's wife, Klara, on December 18, 1918, presumably after Carl's death. The company was closed on June 15, 1919. The Carl Schlegelmilch Company was succeeded by Richard Matthes & Co. (Hartwich, 1984: 27, 28).

The only marks shown in references for the Carl Schlegelmilch factory are ones under the name of Mäbendorf, or Matthes & Co., or Matthes & Ebel, the successor to Matthes & Co. With the exception of one mark, the marks are dated from the late 1920's or 1930's. The marks all include the name "Mäbendorf." None of the marks, including one from 1910, incorporates the name "Schlegelmilch" or the initials "C.S."

China is sometimes found in this country, however, which is marked with "C.S. Prussia" under a clover leaf. The china is similar in style and floral decor to some of the china made by the ES factory. Röntgen (1980: 81) and others have attributed this particular mark to Oscar Schlegelmilch. They have evidently mistaken the "C." for an "O." This mark was noted in my first edition (Gaston, 1980: 26) as an unidentified mark. It will now be attributed to the Carl Schlegelmilch factory based on the information that the company existed from 1882.

The lack of many examples with this mark indicates that little was exported to the United States. The mark also may not have been used for very long. It is even possible that in the beginning, the factory did not mark its china, or that it was used as a branch of the ES factory. Alternatively, the factory could have used some mark which has not to date been documented for the company, or it could have used one of the ambiguous marks which are found on pieces which resemble ES or RS china, but which cannot be definitely attributed to either factory. Perhaps more information on this company prior to the 1920's will become available.

Marks and photographs of the Carl Schlegelmilch Company will be covered in the Fourth Series.

Langewiesen

Oscar Schlegelmilch was Leonhard Schlegelmilch's son by his first marriage, and thus Erdmann Schlegelmilch's grandson. Oscar was not Reinhold's and Erdmann's nephew as stated by Clifford Schlegelmilch (1970: 16).

There is relatively little historical information available concerning the development of the O.S. Company. We saw that from 1885 until 1891 Oscar had been a partner with his brother and father in the Erdmann Schlegelmilch Factory in Suhl. Oscar left the ES company and moved to Langewiesen which was also in

Thuringia. Bad economic conditions for the ES factory probably caused Oscar to leave Suhl. Perhaps he thought he could be more prosperous if he had his own factory. Of course, there could have also been some family disagreement which led to his relocation.

The OS factory apparently was able to succeed while the ES company was failing. The OS porcelain works appear to have been continuously in business form 1892 until 1972. At that time, the factory became a part of the state owned VEB Porcelain Combine Colditz in Colditz (Röntgen, 1980: 436).

The scarcity of OS marked china on the American market supports the theory that little of the production was exported to the United States. Thus, the source of the company's success was not dependent on the large American market. It may have depended more on the local area or the closer European countries. The 1910 Coburg Ceramic Directory notes that the factory employed 300 people. Evidently, it was not a small organization. Table wares and decorative items were produced. The transfer decoration was quite similar to that used by the ES factory.

Marks and photographs for the Oscar Schlegelmilch Company will be included in the Fourth Series.

Tillowitz

Reinhold Schlegelmilch's factory in Tillowitz, Upper Silesia was not established in 1869 as has been reported by most references on the subject. Misinformation from unknown sources at some point in time has been the reason why this erroneous date has been perpetuated. The 1869 date merely reflects the founding of Reinhold's first factory which was located in Suhl. This type of misinformation regarding the founding dates for potteries is not uncommon. Often the date when a certain company produced china is listed as the founding date for a much later company who bought the older one or, who just purchased the plant where china had once been made. Or, in this case and others, the time when a company first started business is used as the founding date for successive operations of that company. Evidently this was a method of adding age and prestige to a later company's production.

Hartwich (p. 23) says that the Reinhold Schlegelmilch factory in Tillowitz had been in business since 1894. The Schlegelmilchs, however, were in Tillowitz prior to 1894. Erhard, Reinhold's son, is noted to have been connected with another pottery in that town about 1887 or 1888. The name of that company was the Graf Frankenberg'sche Factory, noted as originating form the early 1850's. Information from some post World War II refugee newspaper articles described Erhard as working for several years at the Graf Frankenberg'sche Factory before he decided to build his own factory. The Coburg Ceramic Directory of 1893 lists Erhard as Director of that factory.

At some point, Erhard decided the Graf Frankenberg'sche Factory needed to expand, but the owners did not agree. Therefore, Erhard with the backing of his father, Reinhold built a factory in Suhl for the Schlegelmilchs in Tillowitz in 1894. The plant was described as being ready for production in 1895. The factory was located directly on a rail line, making it convenient for bringing in supplies and sending out the finished products. It even had its own rail spur.

The Schlegelmilchs purchased the Graf Frankenberg'sche factory about 1905, because they saw it as competition for their own business. The factory was under the Schlegelmilchs' ownership until 1919 when it was closed and the buildings were turned into apartments. Two marks are noted as having been used by the Graf Frankenberg'sche factory. One is a shield, and the other incorporates the figure of a horse within a double circle. "Tillowitz" is printed inside the double circle. Such marks do not appear to have any connection with the marks used on china by the Schlegelmilch factory they built in Tillowitz. In fact, Wenke (1984: 1) states that the first mark used by the Schlegelmilch factory in Tillowitz was the Steeple mark. The initials "S" and "T" on either side of a church reflected the company's two locations in Suhl and Tillowitz.

Opening a second factory in 1895 in Tillowitz was indeed fortuitous for Reinhold Schlegelmilch. When it became necessary to close the Suhl factory during World War I, the Tillowitz plant was still able to produce. It was available, also, to absorb any left-over stock from the Suhl factory. Moreover, we find that the freight costs were much lower in Tillowitz , the raw materials were closer, and the workers could be hired for much smaller wages.

The Tillowitz factory was quite successful in its production and export during its initial years of operation. Like the Suhl factory, the export trade, especially to the United States was its mainstay. The factory was enlarged early on, and it benefitted from the expertise from some of the best technicians, painters, and mold makers. Some of these had previously worked at Suhl. It is interesting to note that some of the names occasionally found as signatures on the face of some R.S. Prussia marked items can now be matched to the individuals who were either mold makers or painters for the company. (See the next section for the names of these artisans.)

Hartwich (p. 24) says that 1897 was the peak year of business for the RS factories. Economic conditions and the competition from the weapons industry for workers are cited as reasons for the slow down in production in Suhl after that time. Records relating to the Tillowitz factory show that Otto Schlegelmilch joined Arnold, Erhard, and Reinhold as a partner in the company in 1895. In 1922 the company owners were listed as Erhard and Arnold. Arnold had moved to Tillowitz after the Suhl factory closed circa 1917. He is credited with developing an ivory porcelain for the company after that time (Pattloch, nd: 1). This would have been a type of china similar to the English bone china which has some translucency but is not considered true porcelain.

The company's prosperity during its early years is shown by the buildings the company had erected for the town.

Those included a Lutheran church and school, a sports hall, and housing for the employees. The workers were paid in gold and silver coins, and the china produced was described as being the "peak of German workmanship" Pattloch (nd: 1). The company exported its china to many other countries besides the U.S.; Australia, the Balkans, England, Holland, Indonesia, Scandinavia, and Switzerland composed part of the market as well. The Coburg Ceramic Address Book of 1910 lists showrooms for the factory in Amsterdam, Hamburg, New York City, Paris, and Vienna. The 1913 Directory shows that the company had 600 employees. The 1930 Directory lists representives for the company in Berlin, Cologne, Freiburg, and Dresden.

A newspaper article written in 1938 ("Porzellan Kommt aus OS") described how the factory catered to the artistic tastes of the individual countries which imported Schlegelmilch china. The English were said to like elaborate forms and decorations, and Americans wanted complicated shapes and designs. The Dutch preferred a stronger china. The German market was partial to gold trim and did not care for the intricate forms and decorations which were so popular with the English and American markets. Another article (Warzecha) written in the 1950's explained why the Schlegelmilch china was so thin. The American tariffs on imported china were based on weight, thus the thinner the china, the lower the duty.

We know that the World Wars divided by the World Depression of the 1930's were contributing factors which caused the Schlegelmilch china business in Tillowitz to ebb and flow over that time. Where the company was listed as having 600 employees in 1910, the force had been reduced to 400 by 1930, according to the Coburg Ceramic Directory of that year. Erhard, the founder of the Tillowitz factory, and his brother, Arnold, both died in 1934. The control of the company was turned over to Arnold's sons, Herbert and Lothar. Hartwich (p. 23) states that Lothar was the sole owner of the factory in 1941, but his date of death was actually on November 6, 1940. At any rate, after Lothar's death the ownership of the company was inherited by Brigitte Koch. She was the daughter of Christa Koch, Arnold's daughter and, thus, was Reinhold's great granddaughter.

In spite of the tumultous years of the 1920's through the 1940's, the Tillowitz factory was able to stay in business until 1945. During World War II the company also made a type of ware which was called "canteen" china. It was a heavier product, similar to what we might call "hotel" china. It was not the fine, translucent porcelain made by the company prior to the war. The final day of production for the factory was January 23, 1945 (Soppa, 1991). The owner, Brigitte Koch, fled Tillowitz in 1945 before the factory came under the administration of the Poles. She died in Hamburg in August 1991. The Schlegelmilch family was never able to reclaim their property in Tillowitz.

I described in my first edition (Gaston, 1980: 22) the events which caused the town of Tillowitz to come under the administration of Poland during 1945 at the end of World War II. The factory was kept open under Polish administration. One article notes that this was possible because some of the former workers who did not manage to leave the area before it was occupied were given the task of getting the factory back into production. However, this took well over a year to accomplish, which would have been some time in 1947. The china items made by the factory after that time are described as looking "...exactly like those from the time of the Schlegelmilch family" (Pattloch, nd: 1).

The reason for this similarity, however, is probably due to old stock being re-marked or double marked with the R.S. Germany mark or a new mark affixed to previously made unmarked stock. That new mark was the "Made in (German) Poland" mark, reflecting the status of the area which had never been a part of Poland, but after 1945 was "administered" by Poland. As I stated in 1980, the "Poland" mark is post World War II. It was not in use between 1916 and 1918. Those dates have been historically attributed to that particular mark incorrectly. The source of this misinformation is not known, but those years or the 1919-1921 period shown by German reference books on ceramic marks are wrong. According to talks with Herr Soppa by Mr. Capers in 1991, the R.S. Poland mark may have been implemented in order to recapture some of the American market.

The exact length of time that the "R.S. Poland" mark was in use is not known, but it probably was not for too many years. Soppa states that it really would not have been possible for much, if any, new porcelain to have been made in Tillowitz after 1945. The clay needed for its manufacture, kaolin, had always been imported from Czechoslovakia. After the war that country was not interested in exporting this material, because it was needed for the Czechoslovakian china industry. Moreover, the "Council for Mutual Economic Assistance," which was a type of economic union of member countries of the Warsaw Pact, was established in 1949. The council allowed Poland to make only ceramic wares, not true porcelain. Porcelain production was allotted to East Germany and Czechoslovakia. After 1949, china manufactured by the former Schlegelmilch factory in Tillowitz was a type of stoneware, called "Porzellit." Thus, it is conceivable that the R.S. Poland mark was used only during the interval, circa 1947 to 1949.

Chrościcki (1974: 76) shows a new mark instituted by the factory about 1956. The new mark takes into account the fact that Tillowitz was not at that time just in an area administered by the Polish government. It had become a *de facto* part of Poland as a consequence of political settlements at the end of World War II. The new mark bears a definite similarity to the RSP and RSG wreath marks as I described in my first edition. A wreath with the initials "P" and "T" are printed above the words "Tulowice, Made in Poland." A photograph of that mark was not available for my 1980 edition, but the mark will be shown in the Fourth Series, thanks to the efforts of Mr. Capers and the McCaslins. The Poland factory is currently in operation. A portion of the plant burned in 1970, but it was rebuilt (Wenke, 1984: 2).

Marks and photographs for the R.S. Company in Tillowitz other than the R.S. Prussia marks are included in the Fourth Series.

Revised Chronology
of Reinhold Schlegelmilch Marks

Revised Chronology of Reinhold Schlegelmilch Marks

Collectors are aware that quite a number of different marks or variations of marks are attributed to the Schegelmilch factories. In my first two books, I showed photographs of marks found on pieces illustrated. I also discussed other marks which were shown by some references but for which no example was available for photographing. Very little dating information for Schegelmilch marks was available when my first edition was published. I did, however, construct a possible chronology of when the various marks might have been used. This sequence was based on the historical information accessible at the time as well as the type, style, and decoration of pieces with different marks.

In my Second Series I referred to a book on German ceramic marks (Röntgen, 1980) which had not been published prior to my research for the first edition. That author listed some beginning and ending dates for some of the Schlegelmilch marks. These dates were generally broad time periods, such as 1904 to 1938. In some instances, the information did not seem plausible. For example, all RS wreath marks with the exception of RS Suhl have the same time period, 1904 to 1938. In my Second Series I discussed in some detail my reasons for agreeing or disagreeing with the dates listed by Röntgen for both the ES and RS Schlegelmilch marks. (See Gaston, 1986: 9-12.)

I had hoped that for this Third Series more precise dating information for the marks would be found. Although there are several new sources of information, the dates for Schlegelmilch marks are still not clear. Danckert (1984: 11-20) includes a table of marks registered in Germany between 1875 and 1939. A few of the Schlegelmilch marks are found in that table. Basically, these dates are the same as Röntgen showed. But there are even some inconsistencies between Danckert's and Röntgen information. Danckert only shows dates of registration for three out of ten RS marks, and he only shows a registration date for one out of 11 ES marks. A new German source (Zühlsdorff, 1988) notes more registration dates for both RS and ES marks. But there are also some contradictions between his and Röntgen's dates.

I discussed in the Second Series how one cannot merely use a date when a mark was first registered as the beginning date for that mark. Marks were often used before they were registered. Likewise, marks may have been continued after other marks were instituted. In most cases, time periods or a span of some years are probably the best collectors can hope for when attempting to date Schlegelmilch marks. The narrower that time span, the better! I have made a chart comparing the dating information on Reinhold Schlegelmilch marks. The information is based on the three major German sources: Danckert, Röntgen, and Zühlsdorff. I have also included my own revised chronology of marks, which was presented in the Second Series.

Reinhold Schlegelmilch

Comparison of Dating Information for RS Marks				
Mark	Röntgen (1980)	Danckert (1984)	Zühlsdorff (1988)	Gaston (1986)
RS Prussia	1904 – 1938	1905 –	1904 –	mid 1880's – 1910
RS Suhl	1904 – 1932	-----	-----	ca. early 1900's
RS Steeple	1898 – 1908	1898	1894 – 1910	1870's – 1880's
RS Germany	1904 – 1938	-----	1928 –	ca. 1910 – 1956
RS Tillowitz Script Mark R S T Mark in Dotted Oval	after 1932 – 1938 1916 – 1938	1916	1927 – 1932 until 1927	----- -----
RS Tillowitz (wreath)	-----	-----	1932	ca. early 1930's – 1940's
RS Tillowitz Silesia (wreath)	1904 – 1938	-----	1928 – 1940	ca. early 1930's – 1940's
Royal Silesia (wreath)	1904 – 1938	1928	-----	-----
RS Poland	1919 – 1921	-----	-----	ca. 1945 – 1956

From the chart, the differences in the dating information and inconsistencies of that information can be seen. Another RS mark shown by Röntgen and Zühlsdorff is not shown on the chart. That mark is the RS wreath mark with "Erdmann" printed on the left of the mark and "Reinhold" printed on the right of the mark. It is noted as an "anniversary" or "jubilee" mark, evidently commemorating the founding of Erdmann's factory in 1861. The date shown for the mark is 1911.

Danckert, in correspondence with me (see Gaston, 1986: 8) indicated that both factories used such a mark. That mark, however, did not appear in either his 1978 or subsequent 1984 edition. I am sure that this particular mark was misinterpreted by either Danckert or Röntgen from Clifford Schlegelmilch's book (1970). He showed that mark, but I believe that it was only to indicate that both Erdmann and Reinhold used the RS Prussia wreath mark. That was not the case either, however, as I discussed in the Second Series (1986: 8-9).

Danckert does not show any date for the RS (Made in German) Poland mark in his 1984 edition. Röntgen shows the 1919-1921 date which is also incorrect. The RS Poland mark is after 1945 as discussed in my first and second editions (1980: 2; 1986: 12).

There is no conclusive information on when the RS Suhl mark was used. The mold styles and decoration are consistent with the early 1900's. Now we can say, however, that mark was out of use by 1917. Because the R.S. factory in Suhl closed at that time and moved to Tillowitz, a mark incorporating "Suhl" would not have been appropriate. Danckert and Zühlsdorff do not even show that particular mark.

Danckert shows 1905 for the registration of the RS Prussia mark. Röntgen and Zühlsdorff both list 1904 as the date. I still maintain that a period during the late 1800's was the beginning time for the mark. Barlock (1976: 5) talks about catalogs published in 1888 and 1897 offering "a wide variety of stated (R.S. Prussia) china from the Reinhold Schlegelmilch factory." The china, however, was noted as "Not all items trademarked."

In the Second Series I said that 1910 was probably the last year of use for the RS Prussia mark. This date was based on the historical times and events leading to World War I. The Coburg Ceramic Directory shows the RS Prussia mark in its 1913 edition. The mark is shown under the "Tillowitz" listing. The owners of the company are listed as Erhard in Tillowitz and Arnold in Suhl. The banking location for the business is also noted as being in Suhl. This particular listing seems to imply that the RS Prussia wreath mark was used at both the Tillowitz and Suhl factories. This may have been the case during those pre-World War I years before the Suhl factory closed and moved to Tillowitz in 1917.

It is doubtful that the RS Prussia mark was used for any considerable time after the war. The 1930 Ceramic Directory does not show the mark. It does show an RS wreath mark without any town or country name printed under it. It also shows an RS Germany wreath mark as well as an RS Tillowitz, Silesia wreath mark.

The RS Prussia wreath marks which have the additional mark of "Reinhold Schlegelmilch, Tillowitz, Germany" in script form or "Handpainted, R.S. Germany" in gold seem to indicate the transition period for the RS Prussia mark from Suhl to Tillowitz during the "teens" of the 1900's and the few years after World War I. Such examples clearly were exported from Tillowitz. They may have been made earlier, however, in Suhl with the "Germany" mark having been added to old Suhl stock.

The Steeple marks are shown by Röntgen and Danckert as beginning in 1898, while Zühlsdorff shows 1894. I suggested the 1870's to the 1880's for the mark. My dates were based on information that the Tillowitz factory had been founded in 1869. From the shapes and decorations of Steeple marked pieces, I said in both my books that the Steeple marks probably represented an early production of the factory. They do, in fact, represent the first marks of the Tillowitz factory (Wenke, 1984). The Tillowitz factory, however, was not founded until 1894 with production beginning about 1895 (Pattloch, nd: 1).

The 1910 Ceramic Directory has an entry for the Reinhold Scheleglmilch factory in Suhl and an entry for the Reinhold Scheleglmilch factory in Tillowitz. The RS Prussia mark and the Steeple mark (without either "Germany" or "Prussia" printed under it) are shown for the Suhl location. No marks are shown for the Tillowitz location, but in a square where the marks would appear, there is a notation that the factory marks at Tillowitz were the same as the ones at Suhl. This would indicate that the RS Prussia mark and the Steeple mark were both being used at Suhl and Tillowitz.

From studying examples of the china and the marks, it is doubtful that the RS Prussia mark and the Steeple mark were used interchangeable at both locations. It is true that some molds and decorations associated with the RS Prussia mark may be found with a Steeple mark rather that the RSP mark. It is not surprising that the RSP molds and decorations would have been used in Tillowitz, especially during its early years of operation. The question is whether the Suhl factory also used the Steeple mark on its production between 1895 and 1917. For collectors, the only point of significance is that Steeple marked china is probably later than RS Prussia marked china. The Steeple mark was not used prior to 1895. The RS Prussia mark is noted to have been in catalog advertisements from the late 1880's.

The 1913 Ceramic Directory, as noted earlier, lists only a Tillowitz entry for the Schlegelmilch factories and shows only the RS Prussia mark, thus implying that the RS Prussia mark was used in both Suhl and Tillowitz. A few examples have been found with a RS Germany mark and an RS Prussia mark, but to my knowledge no examples with both a Steeple mark and an RSP mark have been found. In the case of the examples with the RSP and RSG marks, we have double marks. The RSG mark is underglaze while the RSP mark is overglaze. This indicates that the RSG mark was the first mark, and the RSP mark was the second mark. Logically, this would mean that the piece was made in Tillowitz, since the RSG mark is underglaze, and the RSP mark was also probably added to the piece in Tillowitz. The question again is whether the Suhl factory also used Tillowitz marks. If it did, such use was apparently limited, because very few examples are found with both the RSP and the RSG marks. Also the Steeple marked china, as well as the RSG marked wares, are generally considerably different in shape and decoration from RSP marked china.

Zühlsdorff indicates that 1910 was the last year the Steeple mark was used. Röntgen lists 1908 as the final year for the mark . The Coburg Ceramic Directory for 1930, however, includes the Steeple mark. The Directory, however, may have only shown the various marks the company had used over time, because several marks for the company appear in the 1930 Directory.

The RS Germany mark is dated from 1904 to 1938 by Röntgen. Danckert lists no date for the mark, and Zülsdorff shows 1928 as the beginning year for the mark with no ending date. I suggested 1910 until 1956 as the time period for the RS Germany mark. Catalog information (Gaston, 1986: 11) shows the RS Germany mark was in use in 1913. From examples, it is logical to assume that the mark was used at the Tillowitz factory for a long period of time. It probably also overlapped with the RS Tillowitz and RS Silesia marks used during the 1920's and 1930's.

I listed 1956 as the final date for the RS Germany mark, because that year was noted by Chrościcki (1974: 75-76) as being the last year the mark was used. The factory was owned by the Polish state after that time. In fact, the RS Germany mark was probably discontinued at the end of World War II when the "Made in (German) Poland" mark was implemented after 1945.

In my first book on R.S. Prussia, I wrote a detailed explanation about the RS Poland mark (Gaston, 1982: 22). Until my book was published, collectors believed the mark was used for a few years after World War I circa 1919-1921. They incorrectly assumed that Tillowitz became a part of Poland after World War I. That particular part of Germany did not become a part of Poland until after World War II. Some references on ceramic marks do show the earlier dates. However, they are incorrect.

The RS Poland marks are not underglaze like the RS Germany wreath marks. The RS Poland marks are glazed over, rather than underglaze. This is an important distinction. Underglaze marks cannot be removed while glazed over marks can be. Porcelain bodies are made and fired first in a bisque (unglazed) form. They are fired again with a glaze which gives the item a glass-like finish. The finish cannot be penetrated. Underglaze marks are applied to the china when it is in bisque condition before the glaze firing. Only single colors can be used in such marks. Underglaze marks on porcelain are found in green or blue. Other colors, such as red, or more than one color (like the RS Poland mark), cannot be fired satisfactorily during that first glaze firing where the bisque body and glaze actually fuse together. After the initial glaze firing, another glaze, even more than one, can be added. These later glazes, however, do not require the same high temperatures that the first glaze does. Thus, such glazed-over marks or decorations can be applied by decoration studios as well as factories. But underglaze marks can only be applied by the factory which actually produced the china.

Although the RS Poland mark is post World War II, the mark is unique as it actually represents the last authentic RS mark. It was not used for very long, from the late 1940's for an indeterminant period of years before 1956. The RS Poland mark is found as a double mark with the RS Germany mark or alone. I noted in my 1980 edition that the mark could have been added to stock already marked with the RSG mark. China bearing the RS Poland mark is often representative of molds and decorations associated with other RS marks.

There is little dispute, except with Röntgen's data, about when the RS Tillowitz and RS Silesia wreath marks were used. Röntgen shows the RS Tillowitz, Silesia, and the Royal Silesia marks in use between 1904 and 1938. He does not show the RS Tillowitz wreath mark, nor does Danckert. Zühlsdorff shows 1932 for the RS Tillowitz wreath mark. He lists 1928 to 1940 for the RS Tillowitz, Silesia mark. Danckert dates the Royal Silesia mark from 1928. I did not show the Royal Silesia mark in G1 or G2, but it is included in the Fourth Series. My suggested dates for the RS Tillowitz and Silesia marks were circa the early 1930's to the 1940's.

Below is my revised chronology of time periods for the major RS marks.

Revised Chronology for Major RS Marks	
RS Prussia Wreath Mark	circa late 1800's to shortly after World War I
RS Suhl Wreath Mark	beginning date unclear, but not before early 1900's; not used after 1917
RS Steeple Marks	circa 1895 until circa the beginning of World War I
RS Germany Marks	circa a few years prior to World War I until 1945
RS Tillowitz, Silesia Mark	circa 1920's to 1940's
RS Silesia Marks	circa 1920's to 1940's
RS Poland Mark	circa after 1945 (probably between 1947 and 1949*) to 1956
PT Poland Mark	after 1956 (and perhaps as early as 1950)*

* These dates reflect the more logical time period rather than that shown by references.

These major RS marks and their variations, with the exception of the RSP mark, are shown in the Fourth Series under the heading of each individual RS mark followed by examples of china bearing the specific mark.

Reinhold Schlegelmilch Marks and Photographs
R.S. Prussia
R.S. Prussia Double Marks
Wheelock Prussia

R.S. Prussia

The R.S. Prussia mark was used by the Reinhold Schlegelmilch factory in Suhl from the late 1800's until 1917 (see RSP Marks 1, 2, and 3). The RSP mark was also on china exported from the Tillowitz factory. While both the Suhl and Tillowitz factories may have used the RSP mark during some of the same time period after 1894 (when the Tillowitz factory was established) and before 1917 (when the Suhl factory was closed), it is most likely that the RSP mark was used in Tillowitz after 1917 for just a few years. Marks 4, 5, and 6 definitely show the RSP mark in use at Tillowitz, because the additional Tillowitz mark is included. The double marks actually seem to represent stock made in Suhl prior to 1917 which was moved to Tillowitz where the Tillowitz mark was added to the RSP mark. The relatively few examples found with both the RSP mark and the Tillowitz mark are further indication that such marks were not used for any long period of time.

The photographs in this section are arranged by Mold numbers and divided into Flat and Vertical objects as in the first and second editions. Quite a few new molds have been included in this Third Series. Some molds, however, have been changed. For example, several molds such as 26, 51, and 339 have been placed under the Steeple marks. Examples are shown in the Fourth Series. Marked RSP examples of Mold 29 are shown under the RSP mark in this book. Unmarked examples will be found either under the RSP mark in this book or in the Fourth Series under the Steeple mark or Ambiguous marks, based on decoration. A few molds such as 401 have been deleted entirely. The decoration is not consistent with that found on RSP marked china. The body of the china is also thicker and not as fine a quality.

Some molds shown in my other two books are not in this edition, because no example was available, or it was unnecessary to show the mold. Thus, there is not a picture of Mold 13, but the status of the mold has not been changed in any way. Collectors should refer to my earlier books for that particular mold. Mold 12 (Lettuce Mold) is not shown under the RSP mark, but it is shown under the RSG mark in the Fourth Series and noted as being RSP Mold 12.

Unmarked examples of various RSP molds are included under R.S. Prussia if there is no question that the unmarked piece matches an RSP marked item in both mold and major decoration transfer. I tallied the molds in my other two books to find which ones had only unmarked examples. When these particular unmarked molds were studied, it was apparent that a few should be deleted entirely, such as Mold 401.

A number of molds not shown in my other books are included in this edition. Caution has been used, however, in placing new molds in the RSP section which are unmarked. A great many examples of "new" molds (that is molds not previously shown in my other two editions under the RSP mark) were sent to me by contributors. Many of those were unmarked, and in only a very few instances a new mold number has been assigned to such pieces.

Some of the other references on Schlegelmilch china show molds which are not in my earlier books. If one of those molds was sent to me by a collector and noted as being unmarked, I included it under the RSP mark if I could document it as an RSP marked example in one of the other sources. That was not always possible, however. The particular mold may have been noted as "unmarked" in those books as well, or the mark may not have been indicated.

The Mold Identification Chart has been reprinted and is shown in an appendix. One major change has been made in the Chart. Mustache Cups have been deleted as a separate category. Those items have been placed under Vertical Objects and classified according to the base shape of the cup. Footed Bowls also have been taken out of the Vertical Objects and placed under Flat Objects.

Some china which has either mark 4, 5, or 6 may have a signature on the front of the piece. "Happ," "Rein," and "Kolb" are some of the names most often seen. Rein and Kolb were mold makers, and Happ was a design painter. These people were brought to Tillowitz from Suhl during the early years of the Tillowitz production (Pattloch, nd: 1). These individuals were professionals in their specific area of expertise. The signatures, however, indicate that the person originally designed the mold or decoration. The signatures do not mean that the piece was made or decorated by that person. Other European ceramic factories, such as Haviland, in Limoges, France, also implemented this practice.

Hartwich (1984: 35) says that printed transfer pictures were introduced as decorations on the china during the 1870's and 1880's. Airbrush decoration was also noted as being started during that period. That particular technique resulted in the shadow flowers and backgrounds which are so common on RS Prussia marked china.

Gold was used to trim and embellish decorations. Sometimes the gold has a copper sheen rather than a rich yellow color. The differences in color resulted from mixing the amount of pure gold with other substances which diluted the liquid paint and changed the color. This was a cheaper method of decorating. It is surprising that so many pieces of RS Prussia, however, do have the rich gold trim. Hartwich (1984: 38) discusses how the workers had to buy their own gold paint. The factory owners thought this would prevent the workers from stealing the gold and also keep them from using too much of it.

The most popular form of decoration on RS Prussia china was floral designs. Many of these transfers have acquired a popular name through common use among collectors. I listed some of those names to describe floral decoration in G1 and G2. In this edition, G3, I have also assigned a Floral Decoration number (FD#) to a large selection of floral designs. Like the Mold numbers, Floral Decoration numbers have been given to those popular named floral designs as well. These numbers should make it easier for collectors to communicate about specific floral decoration on the china.

To organize this numbering system, I did not strictly follow a rule of grouping all of one type of flower together such as roses, lilies, and so forth. I found that was not really needed as long as the major floral transfers were assigned a number. If a piece is described as having FD6, it will be obvious to the reader whether the transfer has roses, lilies, or some other flower. This numbering system has been used primarily for the large floral transfers. The smaller decorations of scattered buds or tiny garland formations could not always be viewed closely enough to easily differentiate among the various ones. Likewise, some of the floral decorations on Vertical Objects were difficult to categorize, because only a portion of the design could be seen on some pieces. Hopefully, the Floral Identification System can be expanded to include the smaller floral patterns in future editions.

A Floral Decoration Index is included for RS Prussia. The Floral Decoration Numbers are indexed to the Photograph Numbers. The captions for the photographs have been written so that the Mold numbers and Floral ID numbers can be easily distinguished from each other as well as from the Photograph number.

The Fruit transfers have also been assigned a Roman numeral for identification purposes. There are relatively few Fruit patterns, but a numbering system for those designs will make it easier for collectors to be able to correctly recognize a particular RSP Fruit transfer.

The marks on the photographs in this book are understood to be one of the RSP Marks (1-6) shown here. The specific mark is not included in the caption. If an example is unmarked, however, the caption will carry that notation.

RSP Marks *also on 187-191*

Mark 1. Red, ca. late 1800's to 1917, Suhl.

Mark 2. Green, ca. late 1800's to 1917, Suhl.

Mark 3. Red with gold "Hand-painted," ca. late 1800's to 1917, Suhl.

Mark 4. Green RSP with red script RSG, Tillowitz.

Mark 5. Red RSP with red script RSG, Tillowitz.

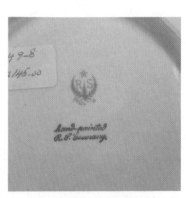

Mark 6. Red RSP with gold RSG and "hand-painted," Tillowitz.

25

R.S. Prussia
Popular Named Molds (Plates 1 through 40)

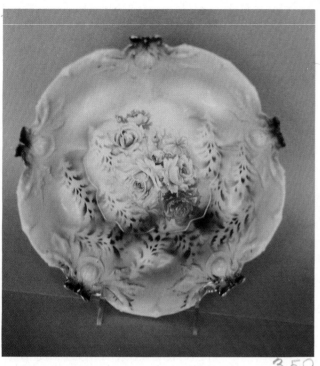

Plate 1. Bowl, 10½" d, Mold 1; Acorn Mold; FD1; roses with blue-green shadow designs.

Plate 2. Bowl, 10¼" d, Mold 1; Acorn Mold; FD2; multi-colored roses with a white rose on a hairpin bent stem.

Plate 3. Bowl, 11" d, Mold 2; Grape Mold; FD3; a pink and a white rose with dark green background on lower half of bowl.

Plate 4. Bowl, 12" d, Mold 2d; Grape Variation Mold; FD21; multi-colored mums and other flowers; Tiffany bronze satin finish on edges; leaves decorated in cream and gold with grapes painted gold.

Plate 5. Bowl, Mold 3; Heart Mold; FD12; white roses with one orange rose; luster finish. 273

Plate 6. Relish Dish, Mold 7; Icicle Mold; FD4; multi-colored roses with rose-colored border. 175

Plate 7. Oval Bowl, 13" l, Mold 7; Swans in Lake scene. 6

Plate 9. *Oval Bowl, 13½" x 6¾", Mold 7; Snowbird scene.*

Plate 8. *Bowl, 8" d, Mold 7; FD 6; pink and white poppies with lily of the valley; blue border.*

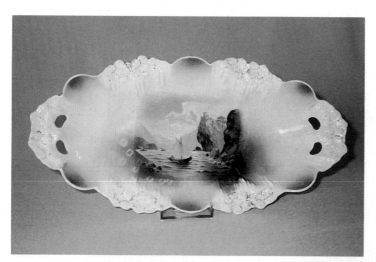

Plate 10. *Celery Tray, 12" x 6", Mold 7; Old Man in the Mountain scene.*

Plate 11. *Oval Bowl, 13½" l, Mold 7; FD6; pink and white poppies with lily of the valley; rose clusters in cameos around outer border; gold finish over stippled designs on border.*
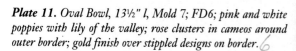

Plate 12. *Bowl, Mold 7a; Icicle variation mold; FD44; Hanging Basket floral decor.*

Plate 13. *Cake Plate, 10½" d, Mold 9; Fleur-de-lys Mold; FD8; multi-colored roses with rose and yellow highlights around border.*

Plate 14. *Cake Plate, 10½" d, Mold 9; unusual gold finish over floral transfer in center; piece is marked with the "Gesetzlich Geschutzt" (patent mark) mark in red as well as the RSP mark.*

Plate 15. *Leaf Dish, 9" d, Mold 10b; Leaf variation mold; FD18; orange and white poppies; irridescent and satin finish.*

Plate 16. *Cake Plate, 9¼" d, Mold 10c; Leaf variation mold; Fall Season figural decor on shaded green background.*

Plate 17. *Leaf Dish, 9¾" d, Mold 10d; Leaf variation mold; FD 13; two orange roses and one pink rose; irridescent Tiffany finish at base.*

Plate 18. *Berry Set: Master bowl, 10½" d; Individuals bowls, 6½" d; Mold 10e; Leaf variation mold; FD13a; pink and yellow roses; irridescent Tiffany finish at base, gold trim. Master bowl has RSP Mark 6; individual bowls are unmarked except for diamond shaped mold mark.*

Plate 19. *Leaf Dish, 12¼" x 6", Mold 10f; Leaf mold variation; Lily of the valley molded design in dish; white satin finish with Tiffany bronze finish on handle.*

Plate 20. *Leaf Dish, Mold 10g; Leaf mold variation; FD23; white flower with yellow center, yellow blossoms, and a yellow rose offshoot; RSP Mark 2.*

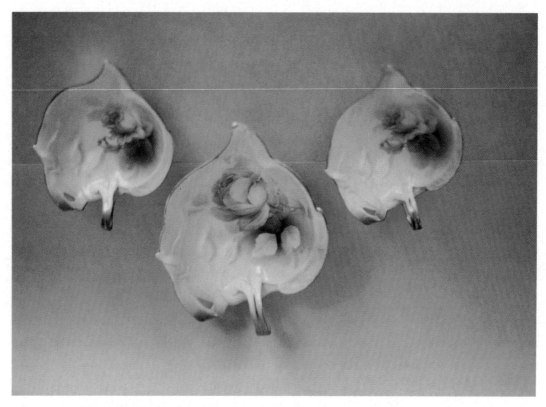

Plate 21. Leaf Dishes, or Nut Set: large dish, 5" l, Mold 10h; Leaf mold variation; FD24; pink-peach rose and bud; molded bud or leaf designs on body of this particular mold; satin finish.

Plate 22. Bowl, 10½" d, Mold 10i; Leaf mold variation; Flora figural decor; unmarked.

1,000

32

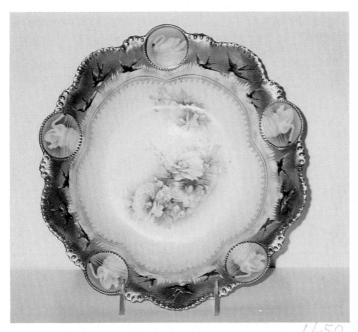

Plate 23. Bowl, 10¾" d, Mold 14; Medallion mold; FD6; pink and white poppies with Lily of the Valley; single swans decorate medallions around border with swallows around wide gold border.

Plate 24. Bowl, 11" d, Mold 14; FD36; Reflecting Poppies and Daises; pink and red rose clusters on gold stippled background decorated border medallions; wide gold inner border; gold trim on outer edge.

Plate 25. Oval Bowl, 14" x 7", Mold 14; Pheasant and Pines scene; medallions are undecorated.

Plate 26. Bowl, 9¼" d, Mold 14; Old Man in the Mountain center scene; cameo scenes of Sheepherder I, Snowbird Scene, and Old Man in the Mountain on border medallions; black inner border overlaid with gold designs; wide gold outer border.

Plate 27. *Oval Handled Bowl, 11" l, Mold 14; FD6; pink and white flowers with Lilies of the Valley; Lebrun I and II, Madam Récamier, and Countess Potocka portraits decorate medallions; wide cobalt inner border; gold stencilled designs frame center; gold trim; unmarked.*

Plate 28. *Plate, 12½" d, Mold 14; FD4; multi-colored rose cluster with one open blossom extended outward; portraits of Lebrun I and II and Countess Potocka decorate medallions; wide cobalt border; gold trim; unmarked.*

Plate 29. *Tray, 11¾" x 7", Mold 14; FD90; Sitting Basket; shadow flowers decorate medallions; gold trim; pearl luster finish; unmarked.*

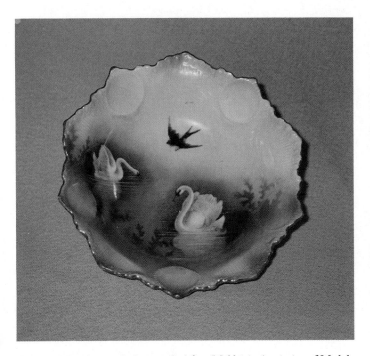

Plate 30. *Bowl, 6½" d, three applied feet; Mold 14a (variation of Medallion mold); Swans and Swallow decor.*

Plate 31. *Plate 8½" d, Mold 16; FD4; shaded green border highlights white plumes.*

Plate 32. *Celery Dish, 12½" l, Mold 16; FD38; Reflecting Water Lilies; unmarked.*

Plate 33. *Celery Dish, 12½" l, Mold 16; cobalt blue finish with white plumes and one floral shape outlined in gold; unmarked.*

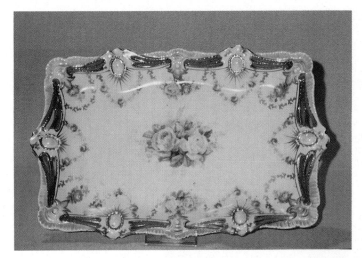

Plate 34. Tray, 12" x 7½", Mold 18, Ribbon and Jewel mold; FD3 decorates center with rose garlands around inner border; pearl luster finish with jewels decorated as opals; irridescent Tiffany finish on the ribbon part of mold.

Love!

Plate 35. Celery Dish, 12½" l, Mold 18; FD38; Reflecting Water Lilies; gold enamelling on lily pad leaves; opalescent jewels; light green outer border.

Plate 36. Bowl, 10¾" d, Mold 19; Sea Creature mold; FD86; spray of pink roses scattered around inner border with FD49a; Surreal Dogwood; dark green border; pearl luster finish.

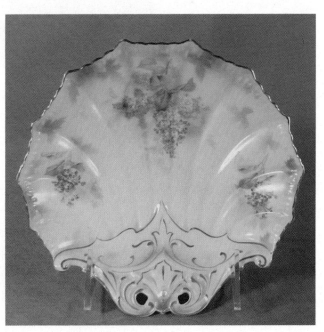

Plate 37. Shell Dish, 7¼" d, Mold 20; FD22; multi-colored flowers in small clusters; gold trim..

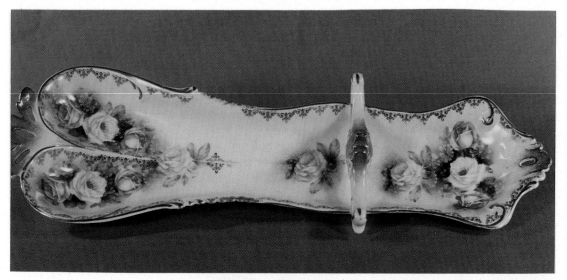

Plate 38. Spoonholder, 14½" x 4½", Mold 21; FD19; yellow, pink, and white single rose blossoms with one yellow rose; gold stencilled designs around inner border; unmarked.

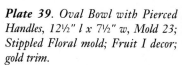
Plate 39. Oval Bowl with Pierced Handles, 12½" l x 7½" w, Mold 23; Stippled Floral mold; Fruit I decor; gold trim.

Plate 40. Oval Bowl with Pierced Handles, 12½" l x 8½" w, Mold 23; FD5; pink roses; dark green inner border; "Klett" signature; RSP Mark 6.

Plate 41. *Bowl, 10½" d, Mold 25, Iris mold; FD10; branch with two pink roses and one white rose; dark green outer border; RSP Mark 6.*

Plate 42. *Bowl, 10¼" d, Mold 25; FD2; multi-colored roses; green inner border; heavy gold work on leaves and outer border.*

Plate 43. *Bowl, 10" d, Mold 25; Summer portrait; Tiffany bronze finish on outer border and Iris designs; white satin finish.*

Plate 44. *Plate, 9½" d, Mold 25; Mill scene; FD7; two open bloom pink roses with two small buds; gold trim.*

Plate 45. Relish Dish, 9¾" l x 4¼" w, Mold 25; Spring portrait; satin finish.

Plate 46. Celery Dish, 12" l x 5¾" w, Mold 25; FD8; multi-colored roses; cobalt blue finish on outer border outlining white Iris; gold trim.

Plate 47. Cake Plate, 10¾" d, Mold 25; FD8; Iris tinted green.

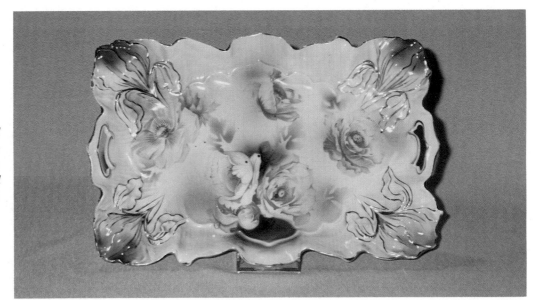

Plate 48. Tray, 11" x 7", pierced handles, Mold 25; FD7; two large and two small pink full blossom roses; watered silk finish around floral designs; pearl luster finish around border.

Plate 49. Celery Dish, 12" l x 5¾"w, Mold 25; Summer portrait with Mill scene in background.

Plate 50. Oval Handled Bowl, 13" x 8½", Mold 25; FD9; four large pink poppies with one blossom closed; rose finish on border.

Plate 51. Cake Plate, 11" d, Mold 25a; Iris mold variation; FD8; gold work on each side of Iris bloom around border.

Plate 52. Cake Plate, 11½" d, Mold 25a; FD25; Magnolia blossoms; deep green outer border; gold trim.

Plate 53. Bowl, 10¼" d, Mold 25a; FD16; multi-colored poppies (colors vary on transfers); black finish around center of bowl with Irises decorated in gold.

Plate 54. Cake Plate, 11" d, Mold 25a; FD26; dark pink and light pink lily blossoms; gold trim.

Plate 55. *Bowl, 9½" l x 7½" w x 4" h, Mold 25b; Iris variation mold; cobalt blue finish shading to light blue; white Iris outlined in gold; floral interior.*

Plate 56. *Bowl, 9" l x 6" w x 3½" h, Mold 25b; rose finish on Iris with wide gold inner border; pink flowers decorate body and interior of bowl.*

Plate 57. *Bowl, 9½" h x 7½" w x 4" h, Mold 25b; FD26; watered silk finish with blue-green color highlighting floral shapes; gold trim.*

Plate 58. *Centerpiece Bowl, 15" d, Mold 28; Carnation mold; FD14; pink roses with one orange rose and white daisies at base of branch decorate center with FD3 around border; gold finish on carnations.*

Plate 59. *Plate, 7¾" d, Mold 28; FD27; a large pink rose with one pink bud; FD3; single pink and white rose blossoms scattered around plate; yellow to cream background; gold scroll work; satin finish on carnations.*

Plate 60. *Berry Bowl, Mold 28; FD28; dark pink and light pink roses; dark green finish around border.*

Plate 61. *Centerpiece Bowl, 15" d, Mold 28; FD25a; Magnolia blossoms with one closed flower at top; shaded blue outer border.*

Plate 62. Celery Dish, 13" l x 6¼" w, Mold 28; FD25a; sand-colored glossy finish on carnations with gold highlights; dark green outer border with shadow flowers.

Plate 63. Berry Set, master bowl with six individual dishes, Mold 28; FD7 with FD26; watered silk finish; gold finish on carnations and outer border.

Plate 64. Bowl, 12" d, Mold 28; Fall portrait. 2,200

Plate 65. Tray, 11¾" l x 7⅝" w, Mold 28; Fall portrait. 2,000

Plate 66. Tray, matching Plate 65, Spring portrait. 2,000

Plate 67. Bowl, 10½" d, Mold 28b, Carnation mold variation; FD15; large multi-colored roses with a small daisy cluster; matte finish; gold trim.

Plate 68. *Bowl, 10½" d, Mold 29; Lily mold; FD16; multi-colored poppies; pearl luster finish; blue-green border with gold stencilled work.*

Plate 69. *Cake Plate, 9½" d, Mold 29; Countess Potocka portrait; gold floral designs around outer border; unmarked.*

Plate 70. *Celery Dish, 12" l x 5½" w, pierced handles, Mold 29; LeBrun I portrait; gold Greek Key border on Tiffany bronze finish; unmarked.*

Plate 72. *Cake Plate, 10¾" d, Mold 29; Fall portrait.*

Plate 71. *Footed Bowl, 10 petal feet, 10½" d, Mold 29; LeBrun I portrait; small enamelled flowers on blown-out shapes around center; gold finish; unmarked.*

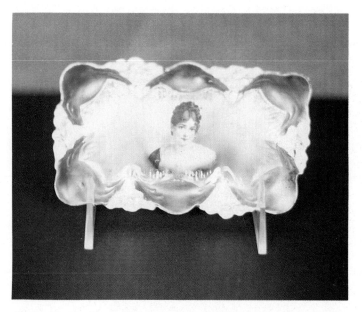

Plate 73. *Pin Tray, 5⅓" l x 3½" w, Mold 29; Madame Récamier portrait; Tiffany bronze finish; unmarked.*

Plate 74. *Relish Dish, 9¾" l x 4¼" w, Mold 29 with handle variation; LeBrun II portrait; gold finish on outer border; unmarked.*

Plate 75. Celery Dish, 12" l x 5" w, Mold 29; FD39; lilac clematis; watered silk finish; unmarked.

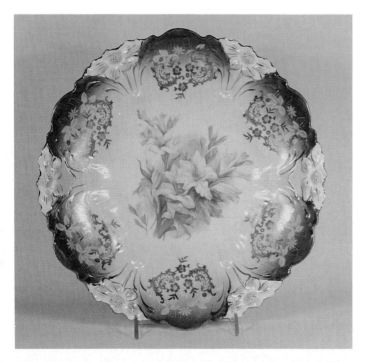

Plate 76. Cake Plate, 11" d, Mold 29; FD29; spray of pink lilies; dark blue outer border overlaid with shadow flowers and surrounded by gold stenciled designs; unmarked.

Plate 77. Footed Bowl, 7¼" d, 2½" h, Mold 30; FD20; pink and yellow open blossom roses with one small pink bud; gold border; unmarked.

Plate 78. Bowl, 10¾" d, Mold 31; Sunflower mold; clusters of tiny pink roses.

Plate 79. Cake Plate, 9½" d, Mold 31; FD17; two large white poppies combined with multi-colored poppies; gold stencilled work around border.

Plate 80. Cake Plate, 11" d, Mold 31; FD43; pair of light and dark pink roses with one light pink offshoot and two small yellow roses; rose finish around border; white satin finish on body; unmarked.

Plate 81. Bowl, 11" d, Mold 33; Bleeding Heart mold; FD16; multi-colored poppies.

Plate 82. Bowl, 10⅜″ d, Mold 53a; *floral border distinguished by double molded blossoms; FD8; multi-colored roses; dark to light green finish around inner border.*

Plate 83. Bowl, 10½″ d, Mold 55; FD2; *multi-colored roses with clusters of daisies; gold stencilled work around inner border.*

Plate 84. Relish Dish, 9½″ l x 4¾″ w, Mold 56; FD25a; *Magnolias with one closed blossom.*

Plate 85. Bowl, 10½" d, Mold 59; large floral blossoms are molded around border and separated by scalloped work; FD16; multi-colored poppies; unusual red inner border; dark green outer border; gold stencilled work; floral cameos spaced around outer border.

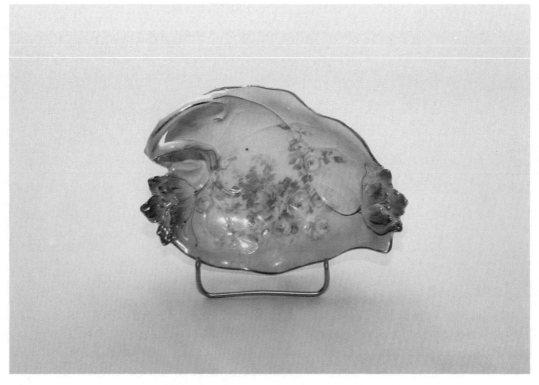

Plate 86. Nut Dish or Card Tray, 6" l x 4½" w, Mold 60; an open flower is molded on two sides of this leaf shaped dish; clusters of small pink roses; pearlized finish.

Plate 87. Bowl, 10½" d, Mold 78; Spring portrait; deep rose finish surrounds dome shapes; gold scroll work.

Plate 88. Cake Plate, 11" d, Mold 78; FD8; multi-colored roses; shaded blue finish decorates dome shapes.

Plate 89. Bowl, 11" d, Mold 78; FD9 decorates center and domes; cobalt blue finish on outer border overlaid with gold stencilled work.

Plate 90. Bowl, 10½" d, Mold 79; FD1 in center with FD7 and FD26 around border; gold trim.

Plate 92. Plate, 7½" d (left), Mold 82; FD28; deep rose finish on dome shapes; jewels decorated as opals; gold stencilled designs; Three Footed bowl, 6½" d (right), Mold 82; FD30; pink rose and white flower; same border finish as plate.

Plate 91. Berry Bowl, 5½" d, Mold 82; FD15; multi-colored roses with cluster of small white daisies; shaded pink finish on body; gold trim.

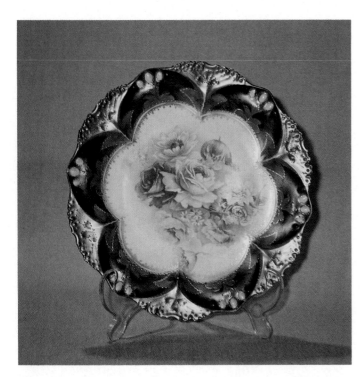

Plate 93. Plate, 8¾" d, Mold 82; FD15; irridescent Tiffany finish; gold outer border.

Plate 94. Bowl, 10¼" d, Mold 82; FD14; pink roses with one orange rose and daisy cluster at base of branch; gold border.

Plate 95. Bowl, 10½" d, Mold 82; FD3; jewels decorated as opals.

Plate 96. Cake Plate, 10¼" d, Mold 82; FD5a; two large pink roses.

Plate 97. Cake Plate, 9¾" d, Mold 82; FD31; Roses and Snow-balls; cobalt blue outer border; gold trim.

Plate 98. Bowl, 6½" d, footed; Mold 82; FD31; Roses and Snow-balls; jewels decorated as opals; dark blue border overlaid with gold.

Plate 99. *Bowl, 6½" d, footed; Mold 82; FD30; pink rose with one white flower; satin finish; gold trim.*

Plate 100. *Celery Dish, 13½" l x 7" w, Mold 82; FD15; red Tiffany finish on domes; gold border.*

Plate 101. *Tray, 12" l x 7" w, Mold 82; FD33; pink poppies and snowball; satin finish with Tiffany accents around border.*

Plate 102. *Oval Bowl, 13" l with pierced handles, Mold 82; Dice Throwers figural decor.*

Plate 103. *Bowl, 10½" d, Mold 82; Flora figural decor with scenes from the Victorian Vignettes and flowers decorating cameos within the dome shapes; gold stencilled work and gold trim.*

Plate 104. *Plate, 9" d, Mold 82; FD34; seven scattered flowers including FD48; a white water lily and a yellow rose; opalescent jewels.*

Plate 105. *Gravy Boat and Underplate, Mold 82; small roses and tulips; green highlights; gold trim.*

Plate 106. *Bowl, 10½", Mold 85; FD8; multi-colored roses.*

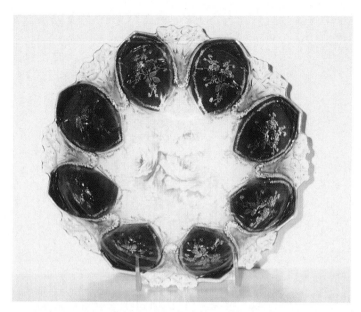

Plate 108. *Bowl, 10¼" d, Mold 90; FD2; multi-colored roses; cobalt blue glaze on oval shapes overlaid with gold stencilled designs.*

Plate 107. *Bowl, 10¾"d, Mold 88; FD3 in center with portrait medallions of the Four Seasons.*

Plate 110. *Centerpiece Bowl, 12" d, Mold 110; castle scene with brown to yellow background; gold trim.*

Plate 109. *Bowl, 10" d, Mold 90; FD9; four large poppies with one blossom closed; shaded blue backgraound.*

Plate 111. Footed Bowl, 7½" d, four feet, Mold 90a; cottage scene with brown to yellow background.

Plate 112. Plate, 8½" d, Mold 91; FD35; dark pink roses with one light pink bloom; dark green Tiffany finish around border; gold trim.

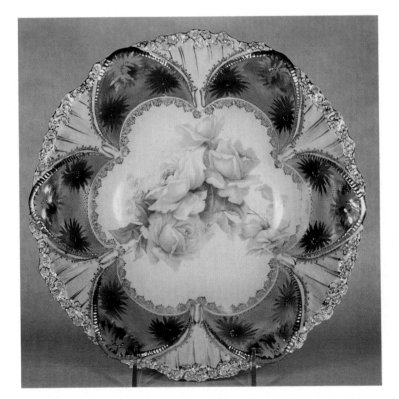

Plate 114. Bowl, 10¾", Mold 91; FD31; Roses and Snowballs; cobalt blue finish on dome shapes.

Plate 113. Bowl, 10½" d, Mold 91; FD11; large yellow roses with one white bloom; cobalt blue and gold work decorate dome shapes; gold trim.

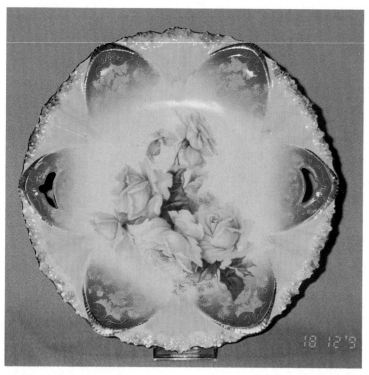

Plate 115. *Cake Plate, 10½" d, Mold 91; FD11; domes decorated with shadow flowers on rose-colored background.*

Plate 116. *Cake Plate, 10½" d, Mold 91; FD33; pink poppies and snowball.*

Plate 117. *Plate, 8½" d, Mold 92; Old Man in the Mountain scene.*

Plate 118. *Plate, 8½" d, Mold 92; Swans in foreground with FD36, Reflecting Poppies and Daisies at top of plate.*

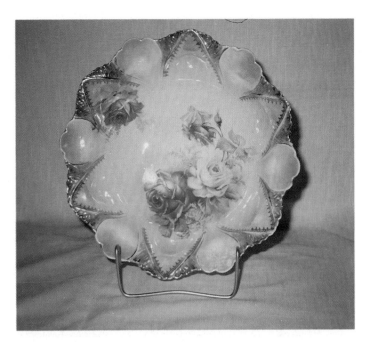

Plate 119. *Bowl, 11" d, Mold 96a; FD37; one large dark pink rose with one white rose and a shaggy pink blossom and bud.*

Plate 120. *Bowl, 10¾" d, Mold 97; Dice Throwers figural scene in center with single Melon Boy in four medallions around border; heavily decorated with gold; unmarked.*

Plate 121. *Celery Dish, 12¼" l x 6" w, Mold 98; Castle scene on brown to yellow background.*

Plate 122. *Berry Set: Master Bowl, 10" d, Individual Bowls, 5½"d; Mold 98; Cottage, Castle, and Mill scenes.*

Plate 123. *Oval Bowl, 13" l x 8" w, pierced handles, Mold 98; Castle scene.*

650-750

6-700

Plate 124. *Oval Bowl, 13" l x 8" w, Mill scene.*

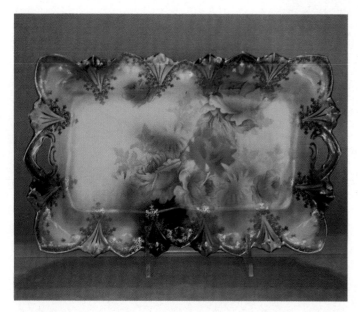

Plate 125. *Dresser Tray, 10" l, Mold 98; FD5a; two large pink roses; watered silk finish; gold trim.*

Plate 126. *Cake Plate, 10½" d, Mold 98; FD39; lilac clematis; shaded dark to light lavender background; unmarked.*

Plate 127. Bowl, 7⅛" d, footed, Mold 98; FD20; pink and yellow open blossom roses; rose finish on dome shapes with a single rose on each; unmarked.

2-230

smaller

Plate 128. Relish Dish, 9" l x 4" w, Mold 98; FD20a; yellow rose from FD20; unmarked.

Plate 129. Bowl, 11" d, Mold 101; FD8; multi-colored roses.

Plate 130. Covered Butter Dish, Mold 108 (base); FD40; bouquet of dark and light pink carnations.

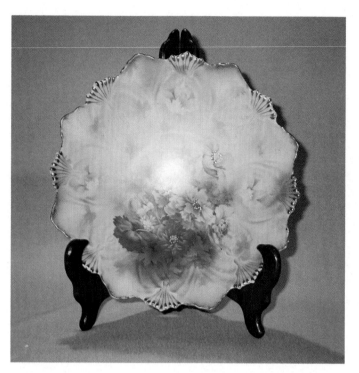

Plate 131. *Bowl, 10" d, Mold 108; FD40; watered silk finish.*

Plate 132. *Plate, 6⅞" d, Mold 108a; dome shapes are not crimped like those in Mold 108; two small pink roses; satin finish; Tiffany finish on leaves and "fan" shapes around border.*

Plate 133. *Plate 8¼" d, Mold 108b; variation in dome shape from Molds 108 and 108a; FD13; multi-colored roses.*

Plate 134. *Footed Bowl, 10⅛" d, 4¼" h, Mold 110; FD46; large pink rose surrounded by white leaves; luster finish.*

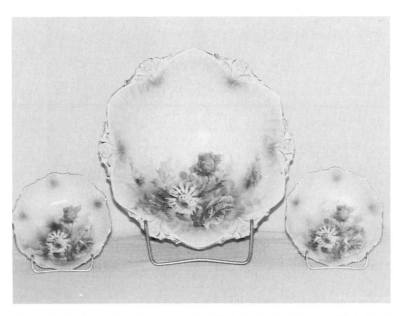

Plate 135. *Berry Set: Master Bowl, 10" d, Individual Bowls, 5" d; Mold 111; six dome shapes divided by a wavy border inset; FD71; one large white spider mum with one dark pink rose and an offshoot of a dark pink rose.*

Plate 136. *Bowl, 10¾" d, Mold 112; eight dome shapes separated by scalloped fan designs; FD41; cluster of small lavender colored flowers; floral design decorates center and also is scattered around inner border.*

Plate 137. *Bowl, 10⅞" d, Mold 113; six dome shapes separated by large lightly scalloped shapes which have molded beaded designs; FD30a; pink rose with one white flower and small daisies.*

Plate 138. *Bowl, 10¾" d, Mold 113; Snowbird scene with white satin finish; pearl button finish on sections separating dome shapes; unmarked.*

Plate 139. Berry Set: Master Bowl, 10" d, Individual Bowls, 5" d, set of six; Mold 114; dome shapes separated by shapes with three scallops with a small fan shape on either side; FD42 on Master Bowl; two large pink roses with three pink buds; FD42a, one pink rose, on Individual Bowls.

Plate 140. Cake Plate, 10¼" d; Mold 115; six blown-out shapes alternate with small lightly scalloped sections; the large blown-out shapes distinguished by embossed floral designs; FD44; Hanging Basket.

Plate 141. Bowl, 10½" d; Mold 116; five recessed dome shapes in center of bowl surrounded by five expanded domes separated by similar smaller shapes; Fruit II decor.

Plate 142. Berry Set: Master Bowl, 11" d, Individual Bowls, 5" d, Mold 151; FD18; orange and white popies; satin finish.

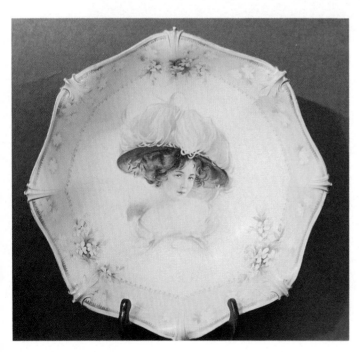

Plate 143. Bowl, 11" d, Mold 151; Gibson Girl portrait; light green border with small white flowers.

Plate 144. Bowl, 9¾" d, Mold 154; FD45; green to brown colored leaves in spray design; satin finish.

Plate 145. *Bowl, 9¼", Mold 155; Swans with Bluebird.*

Plate 146. *Plate, 7½" d, Mold 155; floral branch with two light pink roses and one slightly darker; cobalt blue trim with gold stencilled work.*

Plate 147. *Relish Dish, 12" l x 6" w, Mold 155; FD44; Hanging Basket.*

Plate 149. *Footed Bowl, 6½" d, Mold 158; fleur-de-lys form points around border; FD75; three pink roses with green leaves.*

Plate 148. *Pedestal Bowl, Mold 155; FD74; cluster of multi-colored roses with green leaves.*

Plate 150. *Bowl, 11" d; Mold 159; six large pointed shapes alternating with small, slightly crimped designs; FD15; large multi-colored roses with a small daisy cluster; cobalt blue finish around inner border; green outer border; extensive gold work.*

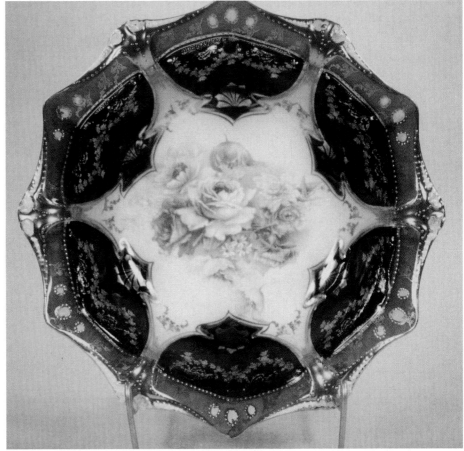

Plate 151. *Bowl, 10¾" d; Mold 182; four reserves bordered with a leaf chain are decorated with cherub cameos or a tiny rose bud; a rose garland forms an inner border with a Tiffany finish on outer border; white satin finish; gold trim.*

Plate 152. *Bowl, 8½" d, Mold 182; three pears (Fruit III), blue-green background; luster finish; unmarked.*

Plate 153. *Oval bowl with pierced handles, 13" l x 8½" w, Mold 182; FD47; white Lilies with Dogwood.*

Plate 154. *Cake Plate, 10" d, Mold 182; Fruit IV decor on yellow to brown shaded background; unmarked.*

Plate 155. *Berry Set: Master Bowl, 10¼" d; Individual Bowls, 5⅛" d, (set of 10); Mold 184; rounded scallops have fan ribbing molded into each section; FD77; large white blossoms tinted lavender at base; gold enamelled work and gold trim.*

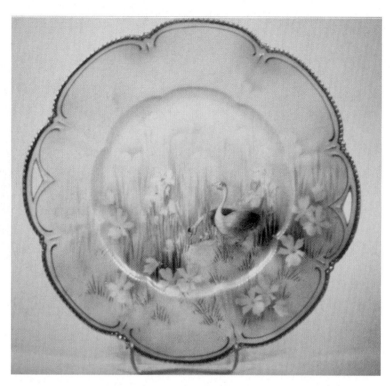

Plate 156. Bowl, 10½" d, Mold 201; FD48; white water lily with yellow rose.

Plate 157. Cake Plate, 10" d, Mold 202; Snow Geese scenic decor with Surreal Dogwood; unmarked.

Plate 158. Plate, 8½" d, Mold 202; Quail scenic decor; Surreal Dog-wood on tan background decorates outer border; gold trim.

Plate 159. Cake Plate, 9¾" d, Mold 202; FD49; Surreal Dogwood with large green leaves.

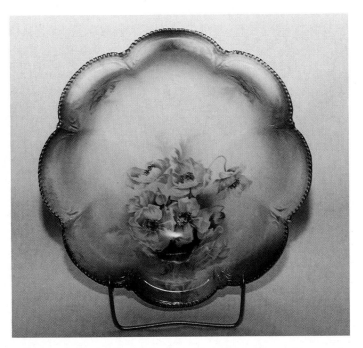

Plate 160. *Bowl, 10½" d, Mold 202; FD17; large white poppies with multi-colored poppies.*

Plate 161. *Bowl, 10" d, Mold 203; pair of Swans; satin finish.*

Plate 162. *Cake Plate, 10¼" d, Mold 207; FD14; pink roses with one orange rose and white daisies at base of branch.*

Plate 163. *Cake Plate, 11½" d, Mold 208; Gibson Girl portrait with FD18; orange and white poppies.*

Plate 164. *Cake Plate, 11" d, Mold 209; small pink rose clusters.*

Plate 165. *Bowl, 10¾" d, Mold 211a; FD8; multi-colored roses.*

Plate 166. *Bowl, 10" d, Mold 211a; Fruit I decor.*

Plate 167. *Plate, 8½"d; Mold 215; semi-round scallops with a jewel in the center; separated by small scallops which have a molded leaf shape; FD14; satin finish.*

Plate 168. Plate, 8½" d; Mold 216; semi-round scallops separated by molded floral designs; FD76; small shaggy pink roses in spray design; satin and pearl luster finish.

Plate 169. Bowl, 10½" d; Mold 217, semi-round scallops separated by smaller scallops with molded scroll shapes around inner border; Swans and Evergreens; luster finish; unmarked.

Plate 170. Footed Bowl, 6" d, Mold 218; rose garlands around inner border.

Plate 171. *Plate, 7" d, Mold 251; FD50; large full bloom dark pink rose; luster finish; gold stencilled inner border.*

Plate 172. *Bowl, 9½" d, Mold 253; FD51; white flowers with yellow pods; gold trim; satin finish.*

Plate 173. *Celery Dish, 13½" l x 7" w, Mold 253; FD11a; one large yellow rose with one white rose; pearl luster finish; gold enamelled work on floral branches.*

Plate 174. *Relish Dish, Mold 255; FD73; pair of pink and white tulips.*

Plate 175. *Relish Dish, Mold 255; FD49a; variation of Surreal Dogwood with gold enamelled stems.*

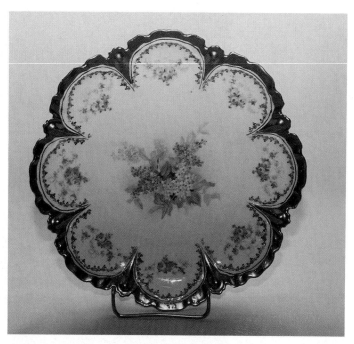

Plate 176. *Plate, 6¼" d, Mold 256; FD49a; pearl luster finish; gold trim.*

Plate 177. *Plate, 8½" d, Mold 256; FD22; multi-colored violets; small rose garlands define shapes around inner border; gold outer border.*

Plate 178. *Plate, 6½" d, Mold 256; FD53; dark pink, light pink, and yellow rose cluster; Tiffany bronze finish around outer center and inner border; gold outer border.*

Plate 179. *Cake Plate, 11¾" d, Mold 256; "Flossie" portrait; green pearl luster finish; unmarked.*

Plate 180. Bowl, 10¼" d; Mold 257a; irregularly crimped scalloped border; cham-
pagne glass with grapes and pears (Fruit V decor).

Plate 181. Celery Dish, 12" l x 6" w, pierced handles; Mold 259;
FD33; pink poppies and snowball; high glaze finish.

Plate 182. Plate, 8½" d, Mold 263; FD55; cluster of three roses
in varying shades of pink; and FD3; satin finish with blue Tiffany
irridescent finish at base of rose cluster.

Plate 183. Bowl, 10½" d; Mold 265a; large scallops alternating with three smaller scallops; FD37; one large dark pink rose with one white rose, and a shaggy pink blossom and bud.

Plate 184. Bowl, 10½" d; Mold 266; irregular crimped scalloped border with embossed leaf shapes molded around inner border; Old Man in the Mountain scene; satin finish.

Plate 185. Small Dish; Mold 267; a shallow ruffle type edge; FD56; Daffodils.

Plate 186. Cake Plate, 10" d; Mold 268; irregular crimped scallop sections form border with small embossed floral designs at four points around plate; somewhat similar to the Icicle Mold; Fruit I decor.

Plate 187. Celery Dish, 12¼" l x 6" w, Mold 276; FD12; white roses with one orange rose; gold stencilled designs around inner border.

Plate 188. Plate, 10" d; Mold 277a; slight variation from Mold 277 on the scroll work around inner border; FD72; one light pink and one dark pink rose with two small buds and two light pink blooms extending from center.

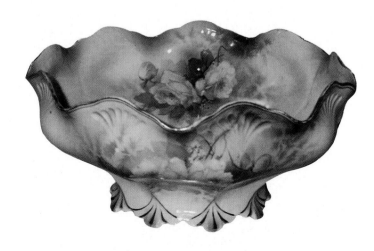

Plate 189. Plate, 8½" d, Mold 278; FD49a; Surreal Dogwood with gold enamelled stems.

Plate 190. Centerpiece Bowl, 10" d, Mold 278; pink roses decorate exterior and interior.

Love

Plate 191. Berry Set: Master Bowl, 11½" d, Individual Bowls, 5" d; Mold 279; large wavy scallops alternate with smaller three section scallops; FD12 with small roses in cameos around inner border; satin finish.

Plate 192. Dresser Tray, 11½" l x 5" w; Mold 281; very shallow wavy scallops form border; white tulips (RSG type of floral decor); RSP Mark 5.

Plate 193. *Relish Dish, 7" l x 4" w, Mold 300; Mill scene with yellow to brown background.*

Plate 194. *Bowl, 10¼" d, Mold 300; FD3; a pink and a white rose with an urn on pedestal; irridescent Tiffany finish around urn; satin finish above urn.*

Plate 195. *Cake Plate, 10½" d, Mold 300; FD14; pink roses with one orange rose and daisies at base of branch.*

Plate 196. *Cake Plate, 11¾"d, Mold 301; FD18; orange and white poppies; satin finsh.*

Plate 197. *Covered Butter Dish, Mold 301 (base); FD70; large full pink rose with bud.*

Plate 198. *Plate, 9" d, Mold 302; FD16; multi-colored poppies; shaded green finish around outer border; gold stencilled designs.*

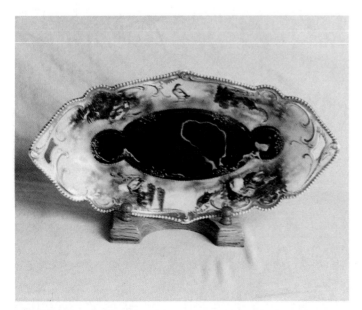

Plate 199. *Celery Dish, 13¾" l x 6¾" w, Mold 304; five Barnyard Animal transfers decorate dish: upper center, Runner Duck; top left, Barnyard Animals group; top right, Pheasant; lower left, Duck and Duckling; lower right, Turkeys and Pheasants.*

Plate 200. *Bowl, 11" d (from Berry Set), Mold 304; Old Man in the Mountain scene.*

Plate 201. *Celery Dish, 12" l x 6" w, Mold 304; FD38; Reflecting Water Lilies; shaded light to dark cobalt blue background; metallic-type finish on beaded edge and outer lily pads; gold trim; unmarked.*

Plate 202. *Plate, 6"d, Mold 304; three scenes: Blue Birds, Pheasant, and Swan; gold trim; unmarked.*

Plate 203. *Cake Plate, 10¼" d, Mold 304; FD36; Reflecting Poppies and Daisies; shaded rose finish around inner border; gold trim; RSP Mark 5.*

Plate 204. *Bowl, 11¼" d; Mold 309a; large five section elongated scallop sections separated by smaller concave sections. (The yellow roses are the same floral transfer found on Steeple marked items.)*

Plate 205. *Plate, 7½" d, Mold 311; FD66; large green tinted leaves in varying shades on vine with small white flowers; satin finish.*

Plate 206. *Relish Dish, 9¼" l x 4½" w, Mold 311; three section elongated scallops alternate with similar smaller sections; FD69; single daisies with laurel chain; pearl luster finish.*

Plate 207. *Celery Dish, 12¼" l x 7¼" w, Mold 311; FD68; two white flowers with one orange flower outlined in gold; satin finish; unmarked.*

Plate 208. *Relish Dish, 6½" l x 4½" w; Mold 312; large indented wavy scallops alternate with small concave shapes; FD67; cluster of white flowers with two offshoots of a pair of orange and pink blooms; satin finish.*

Plate 209. *Bowl, 9" d; Mold 313; large indented wavy scallops alternate with small double fluted sections; FD49a; Surreal Dogwood at top of dish.*

Plate 210. *Pin Tray, Mold 327; FD65; two large pink roses on long stems with green leaves; gold trim.*

Plate 211. *Bowl, 10¾" d, Mold 334; FD44; Hanging Basket.*

Plate 212. *Bowl, 11" d, Mold 334; Turkeys with Evergreens; unmarked.*

Plate 213. *Bowl, 10" d, Mold 340; FD16; multi-colored poppies; irridescent Tiffany finish around border.*

Plate 214. *Cake Plate, 10¾" d, Mold 341; FD54; bouquet of yellow tinted lilies; light to dark cobalt blue finish on lower half of plate.*

Plate 215. *Cake Plate, 10"d, Mold 341; FD62; spray of small light and dark pink roses.*

Plate 216. *Cake Plate, 10" d, Mold 341; Swans with Gazebo scenic decor.*

Plate 217. *Cake Plate, 10½" d, Mold 341; pair of Tigers; rare marked example.*

Plate 218. *Cake Plate, 10" d, Mold 341; "The Cage" figural scenic decor; irredescent dark rose-colored inner border and outer trim.*

Plate 219. *Cake Set: Cake Plate, 10" d, Individual Plates, 6" d; Mold 341a; the smaller scallop sections differ slightly from those in Mold 341; FD63; small yellow and white flowers surrounded by a lilac shadow.*

Plate 220. *Plate, 9½" d, Mold 343; Winter figural portrait in keyhole medallion; deep rose-colored inner border; gold outer border.*

Plate 221. *Plate, 9" d, Mold 343; Spring figural scenic decor m keyhole medallion; irridescent Tiffany purple finish at base of figure; gold finish around portrait decroated with small pink roses.*

Plate 222. *Celery Dish, 12¼" l x 6" w, Mold 346; FD61; two large pink roses with a white leaf; watered silk finish.*

Plate 223. *Small Dish, 4¾" l x 3" w, Mold 347; small pink roses; gold trim; unmarked.*

Plate 224. *Bowl, 10¾" d; Mold 347a; irregular scalloped border varies slightly from Mold 347, but embossed "berry" designs are the same; FD57; one dark pink and one light pink rose with small buds and leaves; dark green finish highlights roses.*

Plate 225. *Plate, 8¾"d; Mold 352; irregularly scalloped border; bust of woman with sheer drape around shoulders and long dark hair adorned with a large flower; blue outer border overlaid with large orange flowers; gold trim.*

Plate 226. *Cake Plate, 9¾" d; Mold 353, irregular scallops incorporating scrolled work on inner border; FD71; light green finish.*

Plate 227. *Bowl, 10½"d; Mold 354; irregular scalloped border in a "ruffle" type design; Flora figural decor with dark green outer and middle borders; gold inner border; unmarked.*

Plate 228. *Berry Set: Master Bowl, 10" d; Individual Bowls, 5¼" d; Mold 355; irregular scallops alternating with ribbed concave shapes; FD23a (Master Bowl); FD23 (Individual Bowls); Master Bowl and one Individual Bowl unmarked.*

Plate 229. *Footed Bowl, 7½" l, pierced handles; Mold 356; irregular scalloped border with fluted scallops on two sides; FD17; gold trim.*

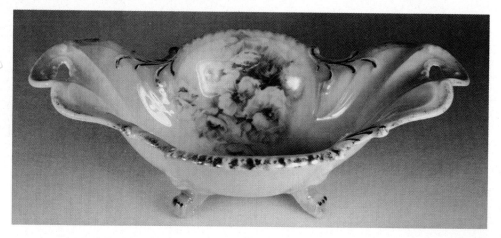

Plate 230. *Plate, 9" d, Mold 404; FD14; roses with daisies at base of stem.*

Plate 231. *Small bowl or nut dish, Mold 404; FD31; Roses and Snowballs.*

Plate 232. *Tray, Mold 404; FD55; cluster of three roses in varying shades of pink; light to dark green background.*

Plate 233. *Oval Tray with Pierced Sides, Mold 427; pink and white fuschias, an RSG decoration; RSP Mark 3 with "Germany" impressed.*

Plate 234. *Tray, 7" x 11", Mold 428; FD59; sprays of small white flowers; wide gold border.*

Plate 236. *Dresser Tray, 7½" x 11", Mold 430; FD59; sprays of small white flowers. This same decoration is found on RSG marked items.*

Plate 235. *Tray, 12½" l x 9⅛" w, Mold 428a; FD64; rose spray composed of a pair of pale yellow roses with one offshoot.*

Plate 237. *Bowl, 10¼" d, Mold 431; FD60; one large pink and one large white rose; satin finish; gold trim.*

Plate 238. *Bowl, 10" d, Mold 432; Mold has two "squared" sides and is not completely round; FD60; RSP mark with "Handpainted" in red.*

Plate 239. *Bowl, 10½" d, Mold 433; FD58; large brown and green leaves with a cluster of yellow seed pods; gold trim.*

Plate 240. *Bowl, 10" d, Mold 434; large single roses scattered around inner border on shaded green background.*

Plate 241. *Footed Bowl, 6" d, Mold 435; FD88 (part of floral transfer), white roses; gold trim; satin finish.*

Plate 242. *Bowl, 5½" h, Mold 436; FD32; a large light pink rose and a smaller white rose; gold stencilled inner border.*

Plate 243. *Pedestal Bowl, 8½" d, applied handles; Mold 437; lilac and white flowers; satin finish.*

Plate 244. *Pedestal Bowl, 10¾" d x 5½" h, Mold 437a (Mold 437 without handles); FD41, cluster of small lilac flowers.*

Plate 245. Chocolate Pot, 9½" h; Mold 451; Cups, Mold 472; FD49a; Surreal Dogwood with gold enamelled stems; pearlized luster finish.

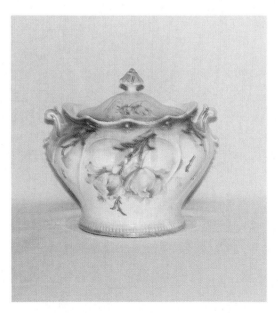

Plate 246. Cracker Jar, 6" h, Mold 452; FD73; pair of pink and white tulips.

Plate 247. Covered Sugar Bowl, 5" h; Creamer, 4" h, Mold 452; Swans on Lake.

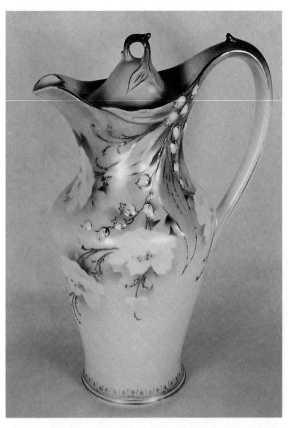

Plate 248. *Chocolate Pot, 10" h, Mold 473 with Lily of the Valley design forming part of body mold; FD49a; Satin finish; unmarked.*

Plate 249. *Demi-tasse Set: Pot, 9" h; Cups, 2" h; Mold 474; FD49; Surreal Dogwood.*

Plate 250. *Tea Pot, 4½" h; Mold 475; FD79, Calla Lily; dark green finish on upper half of body; RSP Mark 8 (see under RSP Double Marks).*

Plate 251. *Tea Pot, 4½" h, Mold 475; FD12; white and orange roses; gold stencilled designs around body and on lid.*

Plate 252. *Humidor, 5½" h, metal lid; Mold 479; octagon shape; FD31a; variation of Roses and Snowballs with flowers in glass bowl.*

Plate 253. *Toothpick Holder, two handles, 2½" h; Mold 480; FD31; Roses and Snowballs.*

Plate 254. *Syrup Pitcher, 4½" h, Underplate; Mold 481; FD66; large green leaves; gold trim.*

Plate 255. *Cracker Jar, 7" h, Mold 482; matches Mold 38 in Flat Objects, Strawberry Mold; FD80; large pink-orange open blossoms; pearl luster finsh.*

Plate 256. *Condiment Set: Open Salt, Pepper Shaker, and Mustard Pot in handled clover shaped tray; Mold 483; small roses decorate pieces; gold trim; rare item.*

Plate 257. *Cup, 2¼" h, and Saucer; Mold 484; FD24; pink-peach rose and bud; white to pale lavender finish; gold trim.*

Plate 258. *Cracker Jar, 3¾" h (lid missing), Mold 485; FD12; white and orange roses.*

Plate 259. *Cracker Jar, 3" h (lid missing); Mold 486; white apple blossoms (an RSG decor); double marked with RSP mark and green wreath RSG mark.*

Plate 260. *Tea Pot; Mold 487; FD85; Lilies of the Valley; gold trim.*

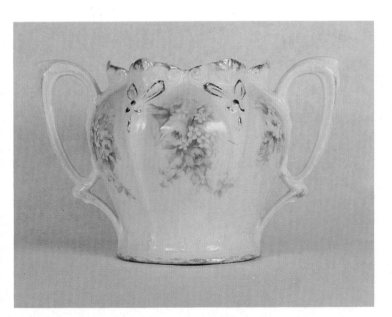

Plate 261. *Sugar Bowl, 3¾" h (lid missing), Mold 488; small roses with white flowers on light green background placed around body; gold highlights and trim.*

Plate 262. *Pitcher, 12" h, Art Nouveau shape; left handed; large white roses with a pearl luster finish; artist signed "Hagmann," non-factory decoration.*

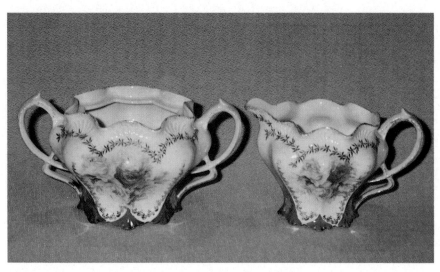

Plate 263. *Sugar Bowl (lid missing) and Creamer, Mold 501; FD53; irridescent rose-lavender finish on base; gold stencilled work on body.*

Plate 264. *Cup, 2¼" h, and Saucer, Mold 501; FD49b; Surreal Dogwood tinted pink-orange.*

Plate 265. *Toothpick Holder, 2⅜" h, three handles; Mold 501; FD53.*

Plate 266. *Mustard Pot, 3" h, Mold 501; FD53.*

Plate 267. *Chocolate Pot, 11" h with two cups; Mold 501; FD49a; Surreal Dogwood blossoms.*

Plate 268. *Chocolate Set: Pot, 9½" h; Cups, 3⅜" h; Mold 501; FD77; large white blossoms with laven-der tint; gold tracery on leaves; satin finish; pot unmarked.*

Plate 269. *Chocolate Set: Pot, 10" h; Cups, 3¼" h; Mold 501; the decoration is handpainted; large pink roses with smaller red roses and green leaves. The set is unmarked, but the art work is of professional quality.*

Plate 270. *Tea Set: Pot, 5½" h; Covered sugar bowl, 4½" h; Creamer, 3" h; Mold 501; FD49b, a pink tint on the Surreal Dogwood blossoms; dark to light blue-green finish; gold trim; unmarked.*

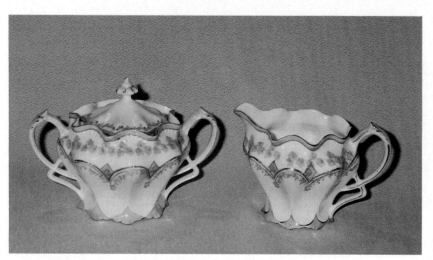

Plate 271. *Covered Sugar Bowl, 4¼" h, and Creamer, 3" h; Mold 501; small ivy pattern around upper border; unmarked.*

Plate 272. Cracker Jar, 7½" h; Mold 502; FD17; large white poppies with multi-colored poppies; lavender tinted base.

Plate 273. Demi-tasse Cup, 2" h, and Saucer; Mold 502; FD90; Sitting Basket; light green finish; unmarked.

Plate 274. Cider Pitcher, 6" h; Mold 506; FD86; spray of pink roses with green leaves; shaded green to cream background; satin finish.

Plate 275. Teapot, 5¾" h; Mold 506; FD22; multi-colored flowers in small clusters.

Plate 277. Cider Pitcher, 6" h; Mold 506; FD86; pale green to white background; lavender and gold irridescent finish around top border.

Plate 276. Chocolate Pot, 9¾" h; Mold 506; FD22; light cream background with green shadow flowers; matte finish.

Plate 279. Cup, 2¼" h, and Saucer, Mold 507; large single roses with green leaves on body.

Plate 278. Cup, 2½" h, and Saucer; Mold 507; FD18; orange and white poppies.

Plate 280. Cup, 2½" h, and Saucer, Mold 507; small rose garlands; gold stencilled work on borders; unmarked.

Plate 281. Mustard Pot, 3½" h, Mold 508; Swans with Evergreens; unmarked.

Plate 282. Cup, 2½" h, Mold 509; pink and white roses on shaded green background.

Plate 283. Cup, 2½" h, and Saucer, Mold 509; pink rose buds; turquoise finish overlaid with gold floral pattern around top half of cup and border of base of cup and saucer.

Plate 284. *Chocolate Cup, 3¼" h, and Saucer; Mold 509; small pink roses; light green border.*

Plate 285. *Mustard Pot, 3¾" h, Mold 509a; small pink roses; light green finish on top part of body.*

Plate 286. *Jam Jar and Underplate, Mold 509a; FD81; white poppies with a pink tint.*

Plate 287. *Cup, 2¼" h, and Saucer, Mold 509a; FD79, Calla Lily; saucer unmarked.*

Plate 290. *Chocolate Set: Pot, 11" h; Cups 3½" h; Mold 510; Swans on Lake; satin finish.*

Plate 288. *Chocolate Pot, 9" h, Mold 509a; FD82; two large white blossoms with yellow centers.*

Plate 289. *Chocolate Set: Pot, 9" h; Cups, 3" h; Mold 509a; FD83; large open blossom white flowers; dark brown finish on top part of body.*

Plate 292. *Covered Sugar Bowl, 4½" h, and Creamer, 3½" h; Mold 510; FD89; pink and white tulips.*

Plate 291. *Chocolate Pot, 11" h, Mold 510; large pink roses with satin finish; unmarked.*

Plate 293. *Toothpick Holder, 2¼" h, three handles, Mold 510; pink rose buds on a long branch; glossy finish.*

Plate 294. *Mustard Pot, 3¼" h, Mold 512; FD87; evergreen branch.*

Plate 295. *Tea Set: Teapot, Covered Sugar, and Creamer; Mold 517; portraits of Madame Récamier and LeBrun I; Tiffany bronze finish.*

Plate 296. *Tankard, 15¼" h, Mold 517; FD5; dark green finish on upper body.*

Plate 297. *Coffee Pot, 10½" h, Mold 517; LeBrun II portrait; green Tiffany finish; unmarked.*

Plae 298. *Tankard, 15" h, Mold 517; LeBrun I portrait; rose finish; unmarked.*

Plate 299. *Chocolate Set: Pot, 11" h; Cups, 3" h, Mold 517; LeBrun II portrait on pot with Countess Potocka and Madame Récamier on cups; rose finish.*

Plate 300. *Chocolate Cup, 2¾" h, Mold 517; FD39; lilac clematis; unmarked.*

Plate 302. *Mustard Pot, 3½" h, Mold 521; large full bloom red rose on shaded green background; satin finish; gold trim.*

Plate 301. *Cracker Jar, 6" h, Mold 521; large white snowballs.*

112

Plate 303. Toothpick Holder, 2¼" h, two handles; Mold 525, Stippled Floral Mold; FD25; Magnolias.

Plate 304. Creamer, 3½" h, Mold 525; FD20; watered silk finish.

Plate 305. Tea Set: Pot, 7" h; Covered Sugar Bowl, 4½" h; Creamer, 3½" h; Mold 525; FD98; one large pink and two dark pink roses with a dark pink rose offshoot on Tea Pot; FD98a on sugar and creamer (same transfer as FD98 except offshoot is a bud rather than a full rose); RSP Mark 6.

Plate 306. Tankard, 13" h, Mold 525; large white flowers outlined in gold on cobalt blue background; stippled design at top decorated in gold.

113

Plate 307. Tankard, 13" h, Mold 525; Cottage scene on yellow to brown background.

Plate 308. Tankard, 13" h, Mold 525; Castle scene on yellow to brown background.

Plate 309. Tankard, 13" h, Mold 525; Madame Récamier portrait decor; yellow to green background with gold leaves and gold finish on top stippled part of mold; unmarked.

Plate 310. Cracker Jar, 5½" h, 9½" w, Mold 525; FD20; yellow and pink rose with one small pink bud; shadow flowers on blue and green backgrounds; unmarked.

Plate 311. Mustard Pot, Mold 525; FD39; lilac clematis; unmarked.

Plate 312. Toothpick Holder, two handles, Mold 525; iris floral design with gold flowers and leaves; gold trim; unmarked

Plate 314. Cracker Jar, 5" h x 9" w, Mold 526; FD26; carnation molded designs decorated in gold.

Plate 313. Chocolate Pot, 12" h; Mold 526; Carnation Mold; FD1; three large pink roses with one dark pink rose.

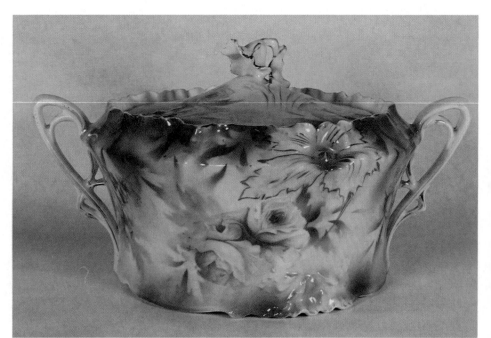

Plate 315. *Cracker Jar, 5" h x 9" w, Mold 526; FD20.*

Plate 316. *Cracker Jar, 5" h x 9" w, Mold 526; FD3; a white and a pink rose.*

Plate 317. *Mustard Pot, Mold 526; FD7; watered silk finish.*

Plate 318. *Chocolate Pot, 10" h, Mold 526; Summer figural portrait.*

Plae 319. Tankard, 13" h, Mold 526; FD7; watered silk finish.

Plate 320. Tankard, 13½" h, Mold 526; Fall portrait.

Plate 321. Demi-tasse Cup, 2⅛" h, and Saucer, Mold 526; yellow-gold and pink roses.

Plate 322. Demi-tasse Open Sugar and Creamer Set, Mold 527; roses with tinted rose finish highlighting body.

Plate 323. Chocolate Set: Pot, 10" h; Cups and Saucers; Mold 454; FD88; cluster of large white roses.

Plate 324. Chocolate Set: Pot, 10½" h; Cups and Saucers; Mold 529; FD84; clusters of purple and white flowers; satin finish.

Plate 325. *Cup, 2½" h, Mold 530; FD73; pink and white tulips; gold enamelled stems; pearl luster finish; RSP Mark 5.*

Plate 326. *Covered Sugar Bowl and Creamer, Mold 534; FD47, white Lilies and Dogwood.*

Plate 328. *Cracker Jar, 5¼" h x 9" w, Mold 537; multi-colored floral decor; satin finish.*

Plate 327. *Chocolate Pot, 10" h, Mold 536; FD5a; two roses form FD5; satin pearl button finish.*

Plate 329. Demi-tasse Set: Pot, 9¼" h; Cups, 2½" h; Mold 537; FD6; pink poppies with Lily of the Valley.

Plate 330. Tankard, 14" h, Mold 537; FD3; lavender Tiffany finish on base and around scroll work on top border.

Plate 331. Tankard, 11½" h, Mold 537; Tigers in jungle setting; dark brown to cream background; scroll work accented in gold, rare marked example.

Plate 332. Tankard, 11½" h, Mold 537; Masted Schooner decor; rare marked example.

120

Plate 333. *Cider Pitcher, 6¼" h, Mold 537; FD25 with rose tint; rose finish at top and base of pitcher.*

Plate 334. *Demi-tasse Pot, 9½" h; Mold 540; Hummingbirds on cream to brown background; rare marked example.*

Plate 336. *Cracker Jar, 6¾" h, Mold 540a; FD47; white Lilies with Dogwood; cobalt blue finish at top of body; gold trim.*

Plate 335. *Creamer, Mold 540a; FD62; lavender tint finish at top of pitcher.*

Plate 337. *Syrup Pitcher, 4½" h, Mold 545; FD49; Surreal Dogwood; pearl luster finish.*

Plate 338. *Chocolate Pot, 11½" h, Mold 550; FD5; RSP Mark 3.*

Plate 339. *Chocolate Pot, 10" h, Mold 551; FD91; spray of pink flowers with a large white flower; tinted lavender finish on top border and base; satin finish; gold trim.*

Plate 340. *Chocolate Pot, 9½" h, Mold 552; FD86; brown Tiffany finish on gold outlined leaf designs at top and base of pot.*

Plate 341. *Chocolate Pot, 10" h, Mold 553 (old Mold 463), Sunflower Mold; FD80; pearl luster finish.*

Plate 342. *Chocolate Pot, 10" h, Mold 553; satin finish with rose highlights; handle decorated in gold.*

Plate 343. *Chocolate Pot, 10" h, Mold 553; FD91; satin finish.*

Plate 344. *Cider Pitcher, 6¼" h, Mold 554; FD47; white Lilies with Dogwood.*

123

Plate 346. Covered Sugar Bowl and Creamer, Mold 556; FD44; Hanging Basket; gold trim.

Plate 345. Jam Jar and Underplate, Mold 555; Castle scene on yellow to brown background.

Plate 347. Covered Sugar Bowl and Creamer, Mold 557; pink and white flowers; blue tinted finish shading to white.

Plate 348. Cup, Mold 558; FD18; orange and white poppies.

Plate 349. *Cup, 2½" h, and Saucer, Mold 559; FD23; satin finish.*

Plate 350. *Mustache Cup, 2½" h, and Saucer, Mold 560; pairs of pink roses on inner border; pink outer border.*

Plate 351. *Cup and Saucer, Mold 561; small white flowers with lilac tinted centers; green outer border.*

Plate 352. *Covered Sugar Bowl, 4½" h, and Creamer, 3½" h, Mold 562; FD25; Magnolias; lavender background.*

Plate 353. *Covered Sugar Bowl and Creamer, Mold 563; FD25; rose finish around flowers.*

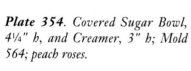

Plate 354. *Covered Sugar Bowl, 4¼" h, and Creamer, 3" h; Mold 564; peach roses.*

Plate 355. *Covered Sugar Bowl, 4½" h, and Creamer, 3½" h, Mold 565; Pears and Grapes, Fruit V decor with small roses and shadow flowers; gold trim.*

Plate 356. Covered Sugar Bowl, 4½" h, and Creamer, 4" h, Mold 566; center cameo of small roses outlined in gold on tinted blue background.

Plate 357. Covered Sugar Bowl, Mold 567; yellow roses; RSP Mark 2.

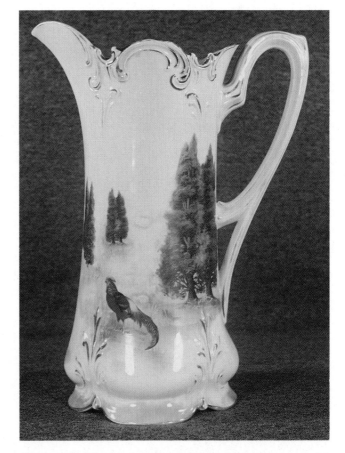

Plate 359. Tankard, 12¼" h, Mold 569; Pheasant with Evergreens; gold trim.

Plate 358. Sugar Bowl, 3½" h (lid missing); Mold 568; Castle scene with dark blue finish at base; gold stencilled designs around top border.

Plate 360. *Tankard, 11" h, Mold 570; Swans and Swallows.*

Plate 361. *Cracker Jar, 7½" h, Mold 571; small roses in garland design decorate body; green highlights around top of jar.*

Plate 362. *Chocolate Pot, 9½" h, Mold 572 (companion to Mold 87 in Flat Objects); LeBrun II portrait; green Tiffany finish; unmarked.*

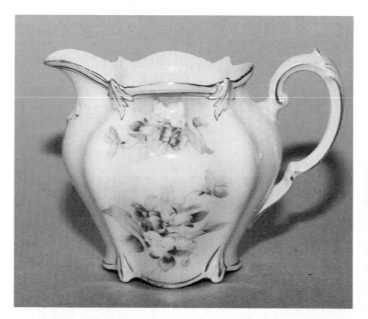

Plate 363. *Creamer, 3½" h, Mold 573; FD92; clusters of purple and small white flowers.*

Plate 364. *Tea Set: Covered Sugar Bowl, Tea Pot, and Creamer, Mold 576; Parrots on yellow to brown background; all pieces marked; a rare example.*

Plate 365. *Shaving Mug, 3½" h, Mold 577; Swans on Lake.*

Plate 366. *Syrup Pitcher and Underplate, Mold 577; FD81; white poppies with a pink tint; gold trim.*

Plate 367. *Tankard, 13" h, Mold 582; FD44; Hanging Basket; unmarked.*

Plate 368. Covered Sugar Bowl and Creamer, Mold 583 (companion to Mold 1 in Flat Objects); Acorn Mold; FD7.

Plate 369. Tankard, 13" h, Mold 584; Bluebirds on yellow to beige background; large white shadow flowers on green background decorate base.

Plate 370. Shaving Mug, Mold 584; Black Duck and Pine Trees.

Plate 371. Coffee Pot, 9½" h, Mold 584; FD6; pink poppies and Lily of the Valley.

Plate 372. Tankard, 12" h, Mold 586; Fruit I decor; dark green highlights.

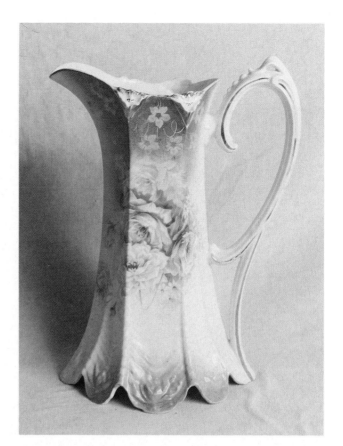

Plate 373. Tankard, 11½" h, Mold 587; FD2; multi-colored roses; pink finish on top and base.

Plate 374. Creamer, 4⅛" h; Mold 588; dark to light green upper border decorated with shadow flowers; small roses on body; gold trim.

Plate 375. Coffee Set: Coffee Pot, 7" h; Covered Sugar; Creamer; Cups and Saucers, Mold 589; raised gold emblems decorate body on light cream background separated by panels of cobalt blue; red finish on top part of body.

Plate 376. *Creamer, 4" h; Mold 602; Swallows; pink tint on base.*

Plate 377. *Creamer, 4" h, Mold 605; FD7; gold stencilled work and gold trim.*

Plate 378. *Tea Set: Creamer, Tea Pot, and Covered Sugar Bowl; Mold 607; FD7; shaded green finish.*

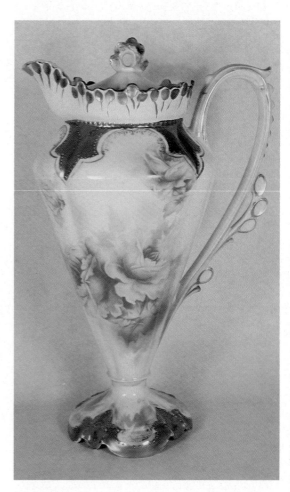

Plate 379. *Chocolate Pot, 10" h, Mold 608; FD5a; gold shield designs with red triangular shapes decorate top of pot; floral designs around top of mold decorated in gold.*

Plate 380. *Chocolate Set: Pot, 9½" h; Cups and Saucers; Mold 608; FD31a; Roses and Snowballs variation; dark green Tiffany finish on base and top border.*

Plate 381. *Cracker Jar, 6" h x 9" w; Mold 609, Fleur de lys Mold (companion to Mold 16 in Flat Objects); FD30; pink roses with small white flowers; RSP Mark 6.*

Plate 383. *Toothpick Holder, two handles, Mold 609; FD8; gold trim.*

Plate 382. *Mustard Pot, Mold 609; FD8; light blue finish; gold highlights.*

Plate 384. *Cracker Jar, 5" h x 9" w, Mold 609; FD8; tinted lavender background; satin finish.*

Plate 385. *Covered Sugar Bowl and Creamer, 5½" h, Mold 612; small pink roses on body; cobalt blue borders overlaid with gold designs; gold stencilled garlands around upper body.*

Plate 386. *Demi-tasse Cup, 2"h and Saucer, Mold 617; FD18; pearl luster finish; gold stencilled designs.*

Plate 387. *Coffee Set: Coffee Pot and Cups and Saucers; Mold 617a; pink roses and white flowers; satin finish; gold stencilled work on borders.*

Plate 388. Cup, 2⅜" h, Mold 318; white flowers; gold stencilled inner border; pink finish on base.

Plate 389. Sugar Bowl without lid, 5½" h, Mold 619; undecorated except for satin finish.

Plate 390. Covered Sugar Bowl and Creamer; Mold 620; molded jewels around top of body and on base; Sheepherder I scenic decor with Swallows; jewels decorated as pearls.

Plate 391. Covered Tureen, 8" h, Mold 621; pink roses with green leaves; satin finish with lavender highlights.

Plate 392. *Cracker Jar, 5" h, Mold 626, Sunflower Mold; satin finish with Tiffany irridescent finish and gold filigree work; unmarked.*

Plate 393. *Sugar Bowl (lid is missing), 3½" h, and Creamer, 4½" h; Mold 627; tiny roses on light blue tinted body; blue Tiffany finish on panels at top of body and on base.*

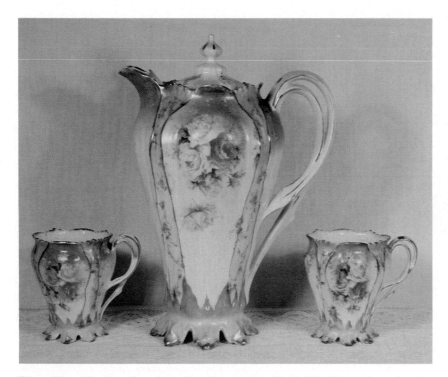

Plate 395. *Creamer, 4⅜" h, Mold 627; cameo portrait decor; lavender Tiffany finish on top panels and base; unmarked.*

Plate 394. *Chocolate Set : Pot, 9" h; Cups, 3" h; Mold 627; FD53; lavender tint at top of body with green finish on base; unmarked.*

Plate 397. *Chocolate Pot, 10½" h, Mold 628; FD8; dark to light green finish.*

Plate 396. *Demi-tasse Pot, 9¼" h, Mold 628; Spring season figural decor.*

Plate 398. *Cracker Jar, 7" h; Mold 628 (Iris Mold); Autumn figural decor.*

Plate 399. Shaving Mug, 3½" h, Mold 631 (Medallion Mold); FD90; Sitting Basket.

Plate 400. Syrup Pitcher, 6" h, Mold 631; Swan decorates medallion with Bluebirds around upper border; FD6, poppies and Lily of the Valley; gold stippled work on top part of pitcher.

Plate 401. Toothpick Holder, 2¼" h, Mold 631; Swallows with Surreal Dogwood blossoms.

Plate 402. Lemonade Pitcher, 6½" h x 9" w; Mold 631 (with smooth base); Old Man in the Mountain decorates front with Swans (not shown) on reverse; black finish on base with gold designs.

Plate 404. Coffee Pot, 9½" h, Mold 631; LeBrun I decorates medallion with gold tapestry finish; FD36 on body; black finish around top and on base; Madame Récamier is on the reverse side (not shown).

Plate 403. Coffee Pot, 9" h, Mold 631; FD36; Reflecting Poppies and Daises on body with FD9 on medallion.

Plate 405. Chocolate Pot, 9½" h, Mold 631; Swans on Lake; black finish at top and on base.

Plate 406. Reverse side of Chocolate Pot in Plate 405; Snowbird scene.

Plate 407. *Teapot, 3½" h, Mold 632; Castle scene; yellow to brown finish.*

Plate 408. *Cracker Jar, Mold 632; Castle scene on jar with Mill scene on lid.*

Plate 409. *Chocolate Set: Pot and Cups and Saucers; Mold 632; Cottage scene.*

Plate 410. *Chocolate Set: Pot and Cups and Saucers; Mold 632; Mill scene.*

140

Photo 411. Covered Sugar Bowl, 3½" h, and Creamer, 3" h, Mold 632; FD3, *a pink and a white rose; satin finish.*

Plate 413. Covered Sugar Bowl, 4½" h, and Creamer, 3½" h; Mold 632a; FD16; *multi-colored poppies.*

Plate 412. Tankard, 14½" h, Mold 632; FD2; *multi-colored roses; dark rose finish decorated with shadow flowers.*

Plate 414. Cracker Jar, 5½" h, Mold 633; Swans with Evergreens; *pearl luster finish.*

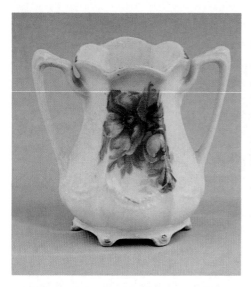

Plate 416. *Creamer, 3½" h; Covered Sugar Bowl, 5" h; Cup, 3¼" h and Saucer; Mold 637; FD18 on Creamer and Cup with FD18a on Sugar Bowl.*

Plate 415. *Toothpick Holder, 2½" h, two handles, Mold 636; FD93; large pink flowers with two buds.*

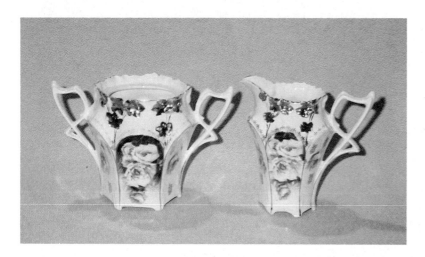

Plate 417. *Sugar Bowl (lid is missing), 4" h, and Creamer, 4" h; Mold 638; FD7 with gold roses; pearl luster finish.*

Plate 418. *Covered Sugar Bowl, 5" h, and Creamer, 3½" h; Mold 639; FD94; cluster of pink and white roses; cobalt blue finish on panels at top of body; unmarked.*

Plate 419. *Coffee Pot, 9½" h, Mold 641 (Icicle Mold); FD38; Reflecting Water Lilies.*

Plate 420. *Coffee Pot, 9½" h, Mold 641; FD44; Hanging Basket; rose colored highlights.*

Plate 421. *Cracker Jar, 5" h x 9" w, Mold 641; Swans on Lake.*

Plate 422. *Cracker Jar, 7½" h, Mold 641; Snowbird scenic decor; unmarked.*

Plate 423. Mustache Cup, 3½" h, Mold 641; FD62; spray of small light and dark pink roses.

Plate 424. Chocolate Pot, 9½" h, Mold 641; pink and yellow roses; unmarked.

Plate 425. Toothpick Holder, 2½" h, Mold 642; FD3; gold trim.

Plate 426. Chocolate Pot, Mold 642; Masted Schooner scene on rust to cream background; rare marked example.

144

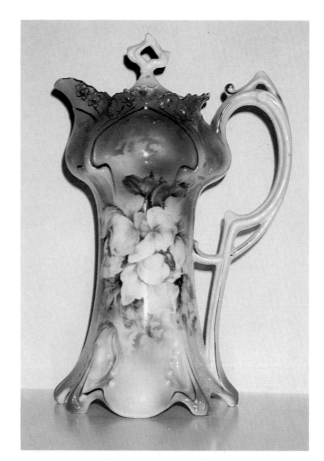

Plate 428. *Chocolate Pot, 11" h, Mold 643; FD25; Magnolias; rose finish at top of pot and around base.*

Plate 427. *Chocolate Pot, 12" h; Mold 642; FD3; jewel decorated as an opal; satin finish.*

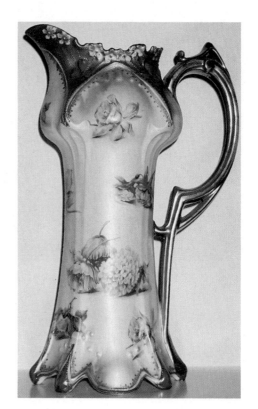

Plate 429. *Tankard, 14" h, Mold 643; FD33; Poppies and Snowball; satin finish with red highlights.*

Plate 430. *Cracker Jar, 7¼" h, Mold 643; Cottage scene; yellow to brown background.*

Plate 431. *Cracker Jar, Mold 643; FD31a; Roses and Snowballs variation; flowers in glass bowl.*

Plate 432. *Shaving Mug, 3½" h, Mold 643; FD31a.*

Plate 433. *Miniature Sugar Bowl, 3" h; Creamer, 2½" h, Mold 643; Single Melon Eater figural decor; jewels decorated as opals.*

Plate 434. *Tea Set: Covered Sugar Bowl; Tea Pot; Creamer; Mold 643; Dice Throwers figural scene on pot with Single Melon Eater on Sugar and Creamer; cobalt blue finish at top and base with gold highlights.*

Plate 436. *Shaving Mug, 3¼" h, Mold 644; FD2; green background with shadow flowers.*

Plate 435. *Cup, 2¼" h, and Saucer, Mold 644; FD7; rose highlights.*

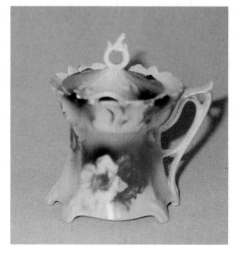

Plate 437. *Mustard Pot, 3¾" h; Mold 644; FD26, a dark and a light pink lily.*

Plate 438. *Cracker Jar, 5" h, Mold 644; FD25; Magnolias.*

Plate 439. *Tankard, 13" h; Mold 644; Winter season figural decor; satin finish.*

Plate 440. *Demi-tasse Set: Pot, 9½" h; Cups, 2" h; Mold 644; FD25; Magnolias.*

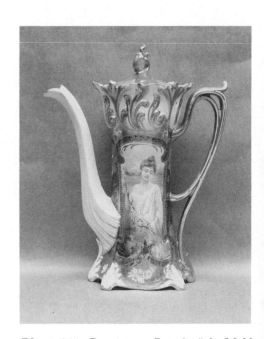

Plate 441. *Demi-tasse Pot, 9½" h, Mold 644; Spring season figural decor; irridescent Tiffany finish with heavy gold work around design; RSP Mark 7 (see next section on Double Marks).*

Plate 442. *Chocolate Pot, 9¾" h, Mold 644; FD8; cream finish with aqua tint on feet.*

Plate 443. *Chocolate Pot, 9½" h; Mold 644; Winter portrait with blue highlights; heavy gold work on scrolled designs; glossy finish; RSP Mark 7.*

Plate 444. *Cracker Jar, 5¾" h, Mold 644; Castle scene.*

Plate 445. *Scuttle Shaving Mug, 3¾" h x 6½" w, Mold 644; small pink roses on shaded green background; RSP Mark 7.*

149

Plate 446. *Chocolate Set: Pot, 11" h; Cups, 4½" h, and Saucers; Mold 645 (Ribbon and Jewel Mold); Dice Throwers scene on pot with Single Melon Eaters on the cups; jewels decorated as opals; heavy gold work. Marked sets such as this, and the one in Plate 447 are quite rare.*

Plate 447. *Chocolate Set similar to Plate 446 except with Melon Eaters scene on chocolate pot; Mold 645.*

Plate 448. Demi-tasse Pot, 9¾" h, Mold 645; Melon Eaters with one figure on each side of pot; jewels decorated as opals; gold beaded work and gold trim.

Plate 449. The reverse side of Demi-tasse Pot in Plate 448.

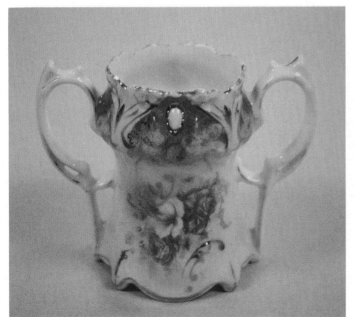

Plate 450. Toothpick Holder, 3½" h, Mold 645; light and dark pink roses with gold scrolled designs; rose finish with shadow flowers on top panels; jewels decorated as opals.

Plate 451. *Chocolate Pot, 10½" h, Mold 645; FD31, Roses and Snowballs; pink border trim with deep rose highlights; jewels decorated as opals.*

Plate 452. *Chocolate Pot, 9½" h, Mold 645; FD26; dark green shading to light green background; jewels painted gold.*

Plate 453. *Cider Pitcher, 6⅜" h, Mold 646; Swans and Terrace scenic decor with brown to rust highlights.*

Plate 454. *Cracker Jar, 5½" h x 9" w, Mold 646; FD95, Canterbury Bells; glossy finish.*

Plate 455. *Cracker Jar, 5½" h x 9" w, Mold 646; FD95; glossy white finish.*

Plate 456. *Cracker Jar, 5½" h x 9" w, Mold 646; FD39; lilac clematis; gold stencilled designs.*

Plate 457. *Tea Pot, 5" h, Mold 647; FD86a; pink roses in spray design varying slightly from FD86; green highlights; gold trim.*

Plate 458. *Covered Sugar Bowl and Creamer, Mold 652; FD86; Tiffany irridescent satin finish; gold trim; unmarked.*

Plate 459. *Cracker Jar, 7" h x 6" w, Mold 652; FD86; irridescent Tiffany satin finish.*

Plate 460. *Chocolate Pot, 10" h, Mold 652; FD86; irridescent Tiffany satin finish.*

Plate 461. *Chocolate Pot with Cup and Saucer, Mold 652; FD96; pink and white spider mums; Tiffany finish around top of body and top border; gold stencilled designs and gold trim.*

Plate 462. *Lemonade Pitcher, Mold 655; Fruit VI decor; sliced oranges; unmarked.*

Plate 463. *Cracker Jar, 5" h x 9" w, Mold 658 (Plume Mold); FD6; deep rose finish with shadow flowers.*

Plate 464. *Demi-tasse Cup, 2⅛" h, and Saucer; Mold 659; small pink roses decorate exterior and interior of cup; shaded blue finish; gold stencilled designs and gold trim.*

Same colors as my
C T Germany
coffee cup

Plate 465. *Demi-tasse Cup, 2" h, and Saucer; Mold 660; FD85, Lily of the Valley on pale blue to white background; RSP Mark 1 on cup and RSG blue wreath mark on saucer.*

Plate 466. *Covered Sugar Bowl, 5" h, and Saucer; Mold 661; clusters of small roses; green finish on base.*

Plate 467. *Creamer, 2⅝" h, Mold 662; pink and white roses on ·cream background decorate reserves which are outlined with gold stencilled designs; wine finish with turquoise highlights on base; gold beaded work and gold trim.*

Plate 468. *Chocolate Pot, 10½" h, Mold 663; FD86; irridescent finish on top border; gold stencilled designs; green highlights on base, handle, and lid.*

Plate 469. *Coffee Pot, 8" h, Mold 664 (old Mold 933); Winter Season portrait; cobalt blue on finish around portrait; heavy gold work overlaid with small pink flowers; spout undecorated.*

156

Plate 471. Cracker Jar, 5" h x 9" w, Mold 664; FD20 on deep rose background; gold trim.

Plate 470. Demi-tasse Pot, 9" h, Mold 664; FD39 on white to cream background; gold panels around top decorated with gold stencilled flowers; unmarked.

Plate 472. Coffee Pot, 9½" h, Covered Sugar Bowl and Creamer; Mold 664; Madame Récamier portrait decorates coffee pot with LeBrun I portrait on creamer and sugar; green tinted finish around portraits; gold trim; unmarked.

Plate 473. *Tea Set: Covered Sugar Bowl, Tea pot, and Creamer; Mold 703; FD85; Lily of the Valley; white satin finish on body with irridescent Tiffany finish on base, handles, finial, and spout of tea pot.*

Plate 474. *Mustard Pot, Mold 703; white satin finish with green tint on base; FD85; gold trim; irridescent Tiffany finish on legs, handle, and finial; unmarked.*

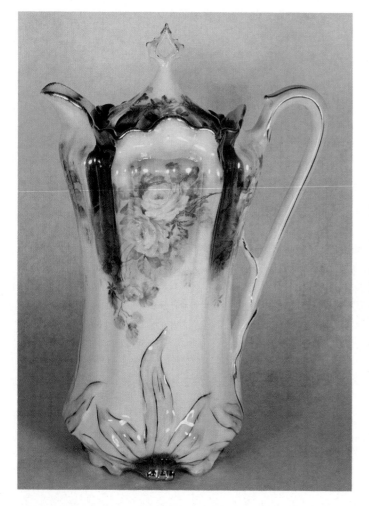

Plate 475. *Chocolate Pot, 9¾" h, Mold 703a (foot varies from Mold 703); pink roses; irridescent Tiffany finsh on panels outlining center decoration and on feet; gold trim; unmarked.*

Plate 476. *Cracker Jar, 7½" h, Mold 703b; FD19; white and pink roses with small floral designs decorating side panels; gold trim; unmarked.*

Plate 477. *Chocolate Set: Pot, 9½" h; Cups, 3½" h; Mold 704; small pink roses; gold stencilled designs with gold crosses applied over floral designs.*

Plate 478. *Cracker Jar, 6½" h x 7" w, Mold 704; FD86b, spray of pink roses on tinted blue to yellow background.*

Plate 479. *Cracker Jar, 6½" h x 7" w, Mold 704; FD99, spray of pink and white carnations; gold trim.*

Plate 480. *Cracker Jar, 6½" h x 7" w, Mold 704, FD100; a dark and a light pink rose with one light pink rose offshoot; tinted green background; gold trim.*

Plate 481. *Cracker Jar, 6¼" h, Mold 705; small pink and white flowers on light green to white background; pearl luster finish; unmarked.*

Plate 482. *Chocolate Pot, 9" h, Mold 706; FD86 with green shadow leaves; body shades from green to turquoise; gold trim.*

Plate 483. *Chocolate Cup, 3½" h, Mold 706; small cluster of purple lilacs on white background with lavender highlights; satin finish.*

Plate 484. *Tea Pot, 6¼" h, Mold 706; gold enamelled flowers and scroll work on white to pale green background; unmarked.*

Plate 485. Cup, 2⅝" h, and Saucer, Mold 706; "Flossie" cameo portrait; green border at top with pink finish on feet; gold trim; unmarked.

Plate 486. Creamer and Covered Sugar Bowl, Mold 707; FD7 on blue tinted background with gold stencilled designs.

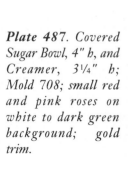*Plate 487*. Covered Sugar Bowl, 4" h, and Creamer, 3¼" h; Mold 708; small red and pink roses on white to dark green background; gold trim.

Plate 488. Hatpin Holder, Mold 728; FD36; Reflecting Poppies and Daisies.

Plate 489. Hatpin Holder, 4½" h, Mold 728; Mill scene with Bluebirds.

Plate 490. Talcum Shaker or Muffineer, Mold 729; Swans on Lake.

Plate 491. Muffineer, 4½" h, Mold 778, FD18 on cream to amber background; enamelled work on flowers; gold trim.

Plate 492. Muffineer, Mold 781; pink roses; Tiffany finish on points around border and base.

Plate 493. Muffineer, Mold 783 (companion to Molds 635 and 807); FD85; Lily of the Valley; semi-glossy finish; gold trim; unmarked.

Plate 494. Hair Receiver, Mold 805 (companion to Mold 507); pink roses on shaded green background with irridescent highlights.

Plate 495. Hair Receiver, 5½" x 4¾", Mold 808 (companion to Iris Mold 25); FD26; rose tinted border; RSP Mark 7.

Plate 496. Hair Receiver, Mold 809; white flowers on cream background; gold trim.

Plate 497. Hair Receiver, Mold 810 (companion to Mold 509a); pink flowers on tinted green background.

Plate 498. Hair Receiver, 3½" x 3½", Mold 811 (companion to Mold 40); small pink roses; floral shape on top painted green ; RSP Mark 1 with embossed "R.S." mark.

Plate 499. Hair Receiver, 4½" x 3½", Mold 812; pink and white flowers; pearl luster body finish with lavender irridescent highlights.

Plate 500. Hair Receiver, 5" x 3¾", Mold 813 (companion to Mold 504, Bow Tie Mold); small pink roses; bow tie painted green.

Plate 501. Hair Receiver, Mold 814; FD49a; Surreal Dogwood; tinted green finish.

Plate 502. Hair Receiver, Mold 815 (companion to Mold 536); small pink roses; lavender irredescent finish.

Plate 503. Hair Receiver, 1¾" h, footed, Mold 816; small white flowers on shaded green to cream background.

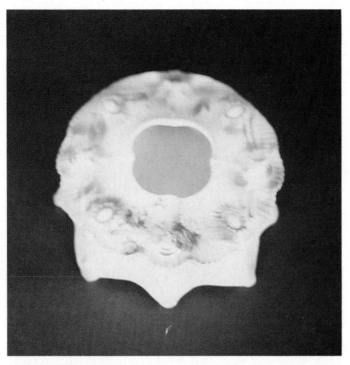

Plate 505. *Match Box, 2" x 4", Mold 826 (companion to Molds 23 and 525, Stippled Floral Mold); FD39, lilac clematis; lavender finish; "striker" under lid; unmarked.*

Plate 504. *Hair Receiver, Mold 816 (Companion to Ribbon and Jewel Mold 645); pink roses.*

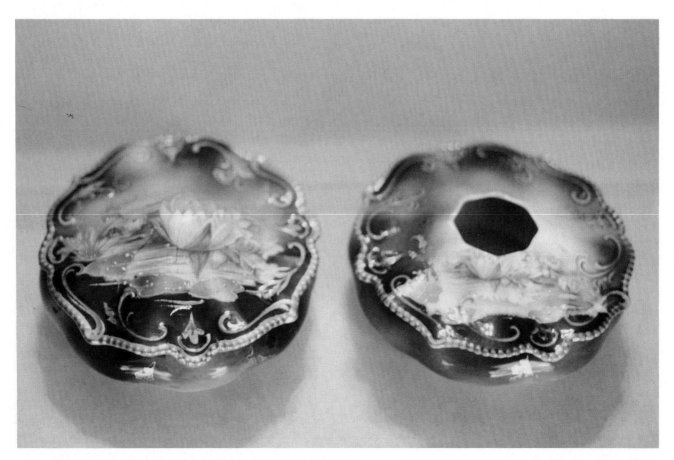

Plate 506. *Powder Box and Hair Receiver, Mold 831 (companion to molds 304 and 584); FD38, Reflecting Water Lilies; cobalt blue background; gold trim.*

Plate 507. Covered Box, 7" x 3", Mold 833 (companion to Mold 728); Black Duck with Evergreens; cobalt blue highlights.

Plate 508. Covered Box, 5½" x 3¾", Mold 834, a double leaf shape; red and white roses on dark green background shading to cream; gold trim; RSP Mark 1 with embossed Star Mark.

Plate 509. Covered Box, 1¾" h, 1" d, a pill or stamp box; Mold 835 (companion to Ribbon and Jewel Mold 645); FD3 with irridescent finish on part of lid; jewels decorated as opals.

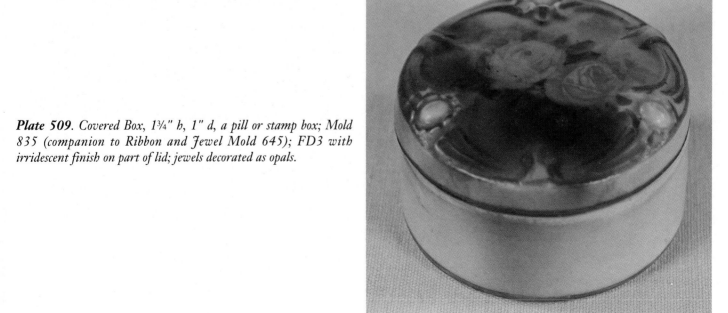

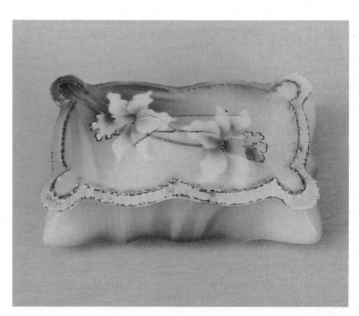

Plate 510. *Powder Box, footed, Mold 836 (companion to Plume Molds 16 and 658); FD44; Hanging Basket; cream background with edges lavender tinted.*

Plate 511. *Covered Box, 4½" x 2½"; three compartments with a hairpin and a straight pin molded in lid; Mold 837; daffodil floral design; gold trim.*

Plate 512. *Covered Box, 4½" x 2½"; three compartments with hairpin and straight pin molded in lid; Mold 838 (companion to Mold 803); FD41; small lilac flowers.*

Plate 513. *Covered Box, 4½" x 2½", Mold 838; pink roses; gold border with gold stencilled designs.*

Plate 514. Covered Box, 3¼" x 3¼", Mold 839 (companion to Mold 40 and 811); white and pink floral spray; gold trim; embossed "R.S." mark.

Plate 515. Covered Box, 5" x 3¾", Mold 840 (companion to Mold 802); small pink roses with light pink shading to white background; gold clover leaf; sponged gold trim; unmarked.

Plate 516. Covered Box, 5" d, Mold 841; FD78; a large white and a large pink open petal blossom with a closed white bloom at top and a small pink flower at bottom.

Plate 517. Candle Stick, 6" h, Mold 853; FD40 on lavender tinted background; a rare marked example.

Plate 518. *Ferner, 6½" d x 3½" h, Mold 879; FD3; gold trim.*

Plate 519. *Ferner, 7¾" d x 4" h (with liner), Mold 879; FD91; spray of pink flowers with a large white flower; gold trim.*

Plate 520. *Ferner, 9" d x 4" h, Mold 882; Swans on Lake; gold trim.*

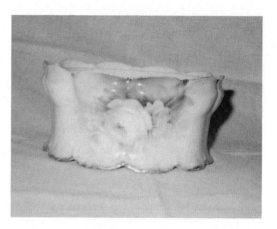

Plate 521. *Ferner, 6½" d x 3⅛" h, with liner (not shown); Mold 883 (companion to Mold 814); FD32; a large light pink rose and a smaller white rose.*

Plate 522. *Flower Holder with porcelain frog; Mold 884; pink and white roses; RSP mark with MW mark for Montgomery Ward Company.*

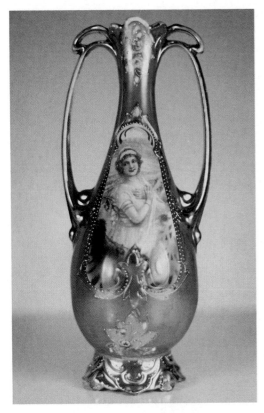

Plate 523. Vase, 10" h, Mold 900; Winter Season portrait; irridescent rose finish; heavy gold work.

Plate 524. Vase, 13½" h, Mold 901; FD3; a pink and a white rose; lavender irridescent finish on base; jewels decorated as opals; gold beaded work and gold trim.

Plate 525. Vase, 13½" h, Mold 901; Melon Eaters scene; red highlights; gold trim; single Melon Eater on reverse (not shown).

Plate 526. Ewer, 8" h, Mold 901; Cottage scene on yellow to brown background.

171

Plate 527. *Covered Urn, 11" h, Mold 903; Cottage scene with cobalt blue finish on top and base overlaid with gold designs; unmarked.*

4,500 PR

Plate 528. *Coverd Urn, 11" h, Mold 903; Mill scene with same cobalt blue finish as Urn in Plate 527; unmarked.*

Plate 529. *Vase, 5" h, Mold 907; Barnyard Animals decorate center of vase framed by gold borders.*

Plate 530. *Reverse of Vase in Plate 529 with Peacock decor.*

Plate 531. *Vase, 5" h, Mold 907; Ostriches on yellow to brown background; unmarked.*

Plate 532. *Vase, 4⅝" h, Salesman's sample, Mold 909; Courting scene on yellow to brown background.*

Plate 533. *Vase, 4½" h, Salesman's sample, Mold 909; Melon Eater decor with irridescent Tiffany finish on top and base.*

Plate 534. *Vase, 5¾" h, Mold 909; Pheasant on yellow to rust background; unmarked.*

Plate 535. *Vase, 4½" h, Salesman's sample, Mold 909; Castle scene; unmarked.*

Plate 536. *Vase, 4½" h, Salesman's sample, Mold 909; Nightwatch Scene with dark green finish.*

Plate 537. *Vase, 5½" h, Mold 909; Mill scene with Swallows; unmarked.*

Plate 538. *Pair of Vases, Sales-man's sample, 5" h, Mold 910; FD7 with gold decorated leaves; satin finish.*

Plate 539. *Vase, 4¼" h, Salesman's sample, Mold 910; Mill scene on yellow to green background.*

Plate 540. *Vase, 6¼" h, Mold 915; Swans in fore-ground with Old Man in the Mountain scene in back-ground.*

Plate 541. *Vase, 9½" h, Mold 922; Swans and Evergreens.*

Plate 542. *Vase, 8½" h, Mold 922; Lion and Lioness; a rare marked example.*

Plate 543. *Vase, 6" h, Mold 928; Hummingbirds on yellow to brown background; rare marked example.*

Plate 544. *Vase, 9" h, Mold 929 (Fleur-de-lys Mold); FD9; poppies; satin finish.*

Plate 545. Vase, 9¼" h, Mold 932; Melon Eaters; irridescent lavender finish with red highlights; jewels decorated as opals; gold embellishments.

Plate 546. Vase, 4¾" h, Salesman's sample, Mold 934; Castle scene.

Plate 547. Vase, 6" h, Mold 935; Hummingbirds on yellow to brown background; rare marked example.

Plate 548. Vase, 7" h, Mold 936; FD3 with lavender to blue irredescent satin finish; jewels decorated as opals.

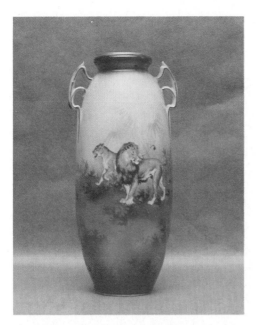

Plate 549. Vase, 11" h, Mold 937; Lion and Lioness decor; rare marked example. #12,000

Plate 550. Vase, 10" h, Mold 938; FD44; Hanging Basket; satin finish; unmarked. 650

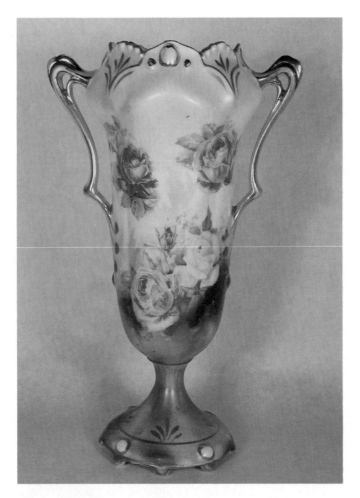

Plate 551. Vase 8" h, Mold 939; FD3; lavender finish on base; jewels decorated as opals; gold trim. 600

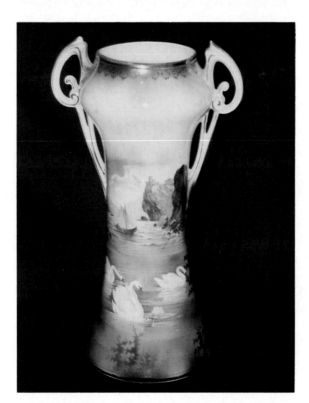

Plate 552. Vase, 11" h, Mold 940; Old Man in the Mountain scene with Swans in the foreground. 800

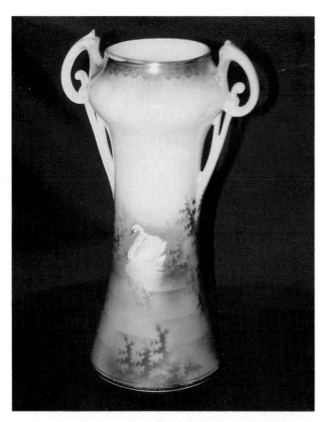

Plate 553. *Reverse of Vase in Plate 552 with single Swan on Lake.*

Plate 554. *Vase, 9" h, Mold 941; Melon Eaters; heavy gold trim; 16 jewels decorated as opals.* $2,800

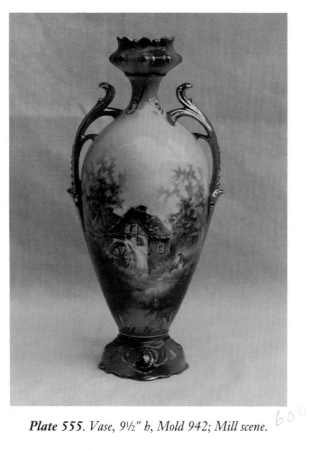

Plate 555. *Vase, 9½" h, Mold 942; Mill scene.* 600

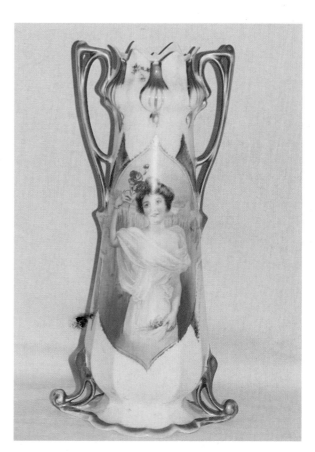

Plate 556. *Vase, 11" h, Mold 943; Summer Season portrait.* 1,200

Plate 557. *Vase, 9" h, Mold 944, an Art Nouveau style with flower molded into body; FD9; poppies with lavender tinted highlights.*

Plate 558. *Vase, 9" h, Mold 944; FD52; a red rose, a pink rose, and a white rose with red center on cream background; lavender to blue tinted finish at top and base; RSP Mark 6 (Handpainted) indicating hand-applied highlights around flowers and gold trim.*

Plate 559. *Vase, 9¼" h x 6¼" w, Mold 945; Flora figural scenic decor on front with Diana the Huntress on reverse (not shown); cobalt blue finish overlaid with gold designs.*

Plate 560. *Vase 9" h, Mold 946; Winter Season portrait; gold trim; dark blue-green finish on top and base.*

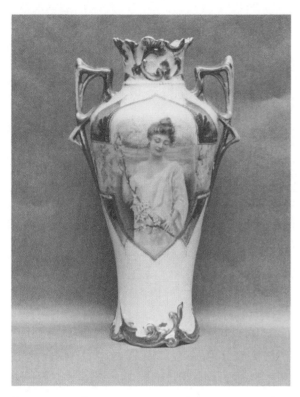

Plate 561. *Vase, 13" h, Mold 947; Spring Season portrait; gold beaded frame around portrait; RSP Mark 7.*

Plate 562. *Vase, 8" h, Mold 948; Winter Season portrait; gold trim.*

Plate 563. *Pair of Vases, 8" h, Mold 949; FD25, Magnolias; gold trim.*

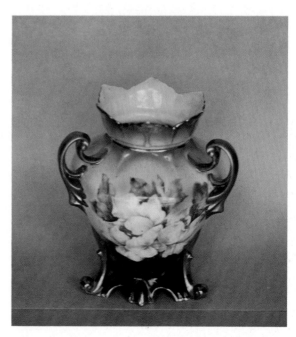

Plate 564. *Vase, 7" h, three handles, Mold 950; FD25; Magnolias; irridescent finish on base; gold trim.*

Plate 565. *Vase, 7" h, Mold 951; Dice Throwers scene; shaded green background; gold trim; two jewels on each side; unmarked.*

Plate 566. *Vase, 7" h, Mold 951; Cottage scene; shaded green background; gold trim.*

Plate 567. *Vase, 11" h, Mold 952; Melon Eaters; 32 opalescent jewels; gold trim.*

Plate 568. *Vase, 8½" h, Mold 953; Spring Season portrait; cobalt blue finish; gold trim; unmarked.*

Plate 569. Vase, 8" h, Mold 954; Winter Season portrait; lavender irridescent Tiffany finish; gold trim.

Plate 570. Vase, 8" h, Mold 955; FD9; pink poppies; shadow flowers on blue to green finish at base; gold trim.

Plate 571. Vase, 13" h, Mold 956 (examples of this mold shown here are unmarked, but the floral decoration is FD39; the same mold is found with the R.S. Poland Mark); Madame Récamier portrait; FD39; lilac clematis; deep rose highlights; gold trim.

Plate 573. Vase, 5" h, Mold 957; floral decor overlaid with tapestry finish.

Plate 572. Vase, 10" h, Mold 956; LeBrun I portrait; green finish at top and base; pearl luster finish on body; opalescent jewels decorate base; gold trim; unmarked.

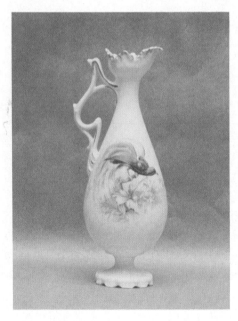

Plate 575. Ewer, 7¼" x 5½", Mold 959; FD52; a red rose, a pink rose, and a white rose with red center; cream background; lavender to blue finish at top and base; gold trim; RSP Mark 6.

Plate 574. Ewer, 7½" h, Mold 958; Bird of Paradise on white satin finish; rare marked example.

Plate 576. *Ewer, 7¼" x 5½", Mold 959; Diana the Huntress on front with Flora on reverse; cobalt blue finish; gold trim; unmarked.*

Plate 577. *Reverse of Ewer in Plate 576.*

Plate 578. *Vase, 11½" h, Mold 960; LeBrun II portrait; cobalt blue finish at top, base, and around portrait; gold enamelled work and gold trim; unmarked.*

Plate 579. *Vase, 9¼" h, Mold 960; Madame Récamier portrait; FD39; lilac clematis at base of portrait; deep rose highlights; gold trim; unmarked.*

Plate 580. *Potpourri Jar, 9" h, (lid is pierced), Mold 961; Countess Potocka portrait; FD39 at base; colors in finish are the same as Vase in Plate 579; unmarked.*

Plate 581. *Covered Urn, 11" h, Mold 962; "The Cage" figural decor; wine finish overlaid with gold stencilled designs.*

Plate 583. *Covered Urn, 12" h, Mold 964; Dice Throwers scene; shaded blue to green finish; 14 opalescent jewels.*

Plate 582. *Covered Urn, 9¾" h, Mold 963 (companion to Ribbon and Jewel molds); single Melon Eater; opalescent jewels; heavy gold trim.*

R.S. Prussia Double Marks

The R.S. Prussia mark may be accompanied by another mark. The explanation for the second mark may be obvious. Names of American importers are sometimes found with the R.S. Prussia mark. Such marks are usually printed marks, but paper labels were used as well as is shown in one example. Adding an American importer's mark was a common practice for European ceramic factories during the late 1800's and early 1900's.

"Gesetzlich Geschutzt" is frequently found with the R.S. Prussia mark. The German words are comparable to "patented" or "trade mark."

Several other marks which are occasionally found with the R.S. Prussia mark are not easily explained. There is no doubt that the china was made by the R.S. Schlegelmilch factory. The molds are Schlegelmilch molds, and the floral decorations are transfers commonly found on Schlegelmilch molds or very similar to them. The R.S. Prussia mark on the pieces, of course, erases any question that the china was made by the R.S. factory.

These double marks are rather fancy in most cases and usually include "Royal" as part of the mark. The reason for such marks is not known. In all likelihood, the various "Royal" marks were added to the R.S. Prussia mark merely to impart a look of prestige. The use of "Royal" and "Imperial" in a ceramic mark does not indicate that the china was made for royalty. This type of rumor is often associated with such marks. A number of examples are shown in the following photographs.

RSP Mark 7 with "Gesetzlich Geschutzt" (patent mark) in gold.

RSP Mark 8 with "BT Co GERMANY" in gold. (The BT mark may refer to Burley Tyrrell an American importing firm. The BT mark is also found as a single mark or with the R.S. Germany mark.)

RSP Mark 9 with a paper label for the J.C. Markert company of Marion, Ohio.

RSP Mark 10 with gold "Dresden" mark.

RSP Mark 11 with "Imperial Bremen Porcelain."

Plate 584. *Plate, 6¼" d, Mold is a companion to RSP Mold 506; shaggy pink roses; gold stencilled designs; gold trim; RSP Mark 11.*

RSP Mark 12 with "Royal Chemnitz" in gold.

Plate 585. *Sugar Bowl (lid is missing), 3¾" h, Mold 509a; FD79; Calla Lily; pearl luster finish; RSP Mark 12.*

RSP Mark 13 with "Royal Hamburg" in gold.

Plate 586. *Individual Berry Bowl, Mold 202; cluster of pink roses; RSP Mark 13.*

RSP Mark 14 with Crown and "Metz" in gold.

Plate 587. Cake Plate, 10" d, Mold 333; same floral transfer as shown in Plate 586; gold trim; RSP Mark 14.

RSP Mark 15 with "Royal Pomerania" in gold.

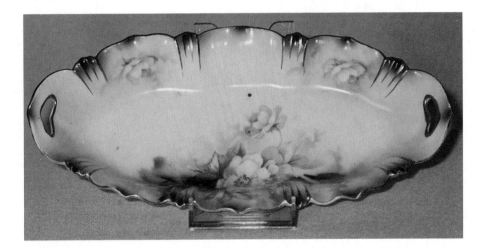

Plate 588. Relish Dish, 8" h; companion to RSP Mold 503; FD23; RSP Mark 15.

RSP 16 with "Royal Strassburg" in gold.

Plate 589. Covered Sugar Bowl, 7" h; Mold 507; pink roses with shadow flowers and garlands decorate body; RSP Mark 16.

189

RSP Mark 17 with "Royal Vienna" in gold. No examples shown in this Series.

RSP Mark 18 with "Royal Wittenberg" in gold.

Plate 590. Plate, 8" d; Mold 303; FD18; RSP Mark 18.

RSP Mark 19 with "Royal Zitteu" in gold.

Plate 591. Plate, 6½" d; Mold 305, lavender and white flowers; RSP Mark 19.

Wheelock Prussia

The "Wheelock" Prussia mark was explained in the Second Series. The mark was used by an Illinois based company which imported china to the United States. This method of substituting an importer's mark for the factory mark was not unusual for European china factories. The lettering of "Prussia" underneath the mark is the same color and style of print as "Prussia" in the R.S. mark.

The Wheelock mark without "Prussia" was registered in 1914 although the company indicated that it had been used since 1898 (Lehner, 1988: 518). The Wheelock Prussia mark, therefore, would not have been used prior to 1898.

The Wheelock mark is found on RSP molds. The decoration transfers are ones commonly associated with R.S. Prussia marked china. Collectors should realize that Wheelock Prussia and Schlegelmilch china are one and the same. Value for the Wheelock marked pieces should be comparable to R.S. Prussia marked china if the pieces are documented RSP molds with RSP decoration themes.

Wheelock Prussia Mark 1

Wheelock Prussia Mark 2 with "handpainted R.S. Germany" in gold.

Plate 592. *Covered Sugar Bowl, 5¼" h; RSP Mold 600; two turkeys decorate front with one turkey on back (not shown); cobalt blue finish at top and base; gold stencilled designs; Wheelock Prussia Mark 1.*

Plate 593. *Relish Dish, 9¾" l, RSP Mold 9; pink roses on tinted pink background; satin finish; gold trim; Wheelock Prussia Mark 2.*

Plate 594. *Bowl, Mold 7; Swans on Lake; Wheelock Prussia Mark 1.*

Plate 595. *Tankard, 12" h, RSP Mold 586; red poinsettias with dark green highlights; gold trim; Wheelock Prussia Mark 1.*

Bibliography

Adressbuch der Keram-Industrie. Coburg: Müller & Schmidt, 1893, 1910, 1913, 1930, 1932, 1934, 1937, 1941, 1949.

Ananoff, Alexandre, *L'oeuvre Dessiné* de Francois Boucher. Paris: F. De Nobele, Librarie, 1966.

Barber, Edwin Atlee, *The Ceramic Collectors' Glossary*. New York: Da Capo Press, 1967.

Barlock, George E. and Eileen. *The Treasures of R.S. Prussia*, 1976.

Bartran, Margaret. *A Guide to Color Reproductions*. Second Edition. Metuchen, NJ: The Scarecrow Press, Inc., 1971.

Bearne, Mrs. *A Court Painter and His Circle, Francois Boucher*. London: Adelphi Terrace, 1913.

Benson, E.F. *The White Eagle of Poland*. New York: George H. Doran Company, n.d.

Boger, Louise Ade. *The Dictionary of World Pottery and Porcelain*. New York: Charles Scribner's Sons, 1971

Buell, Raymond Leslie. *Poland: Key to Europe*. London: Jonathan Cape, 1939.

Calvert, Albert F. (ed.). *Murillo: The Spanish Series*. London: John Lane, The Bodley Head Gallery, MCMVII.

Capers, R.H. Discussions with Gerhard Soppa, November 26 and 27, 1991.

_____. "R.S. Made in (German) Poland" Mark, *R.S. Prussia* (Number 16, Febuary, 1992): 8-10.

Castries, Duc de. *Madame Récamier*. Hachette, 1971.

Catalogue of Reproductions of Paintings Prior to 1860. Paris: UNESCO, 1972.

Chaffers, William. *Handbook of Marks and Monograms on Pottery and Porcelain*. Revised edition. London: William Reeves, 1968.

_____. *Marks & Monograms on Pottery and Porcelain*. Vol. 1, 15th Revised edition. London: William Reeves, 1965.

Chrościcki, Leon. *Porcelana — Znaki Wytworni Europejskich*. Warszawa: Wybawnictwo Artystyczno-Graficzne, 1974.

Cox, W.E. *The Book of Pottery and Porcelain*. Vol. 1. New York: L. Lee Shepard Co., Inc., 1944.

Cushion, J.P. *Pocket Book of German Ceramic Marks and Those of Other Central European Countries*. London: Faber and Faber, 1961.

Cushion, J.P. (in collaboration with W.B. Honey). *Handbook of Pottery and Porcelain Marks*. London: Faber & Faber, 1956.

Danckert, Ludwig. *Hanbuch des Europäischen Porzellans*. Munich: Prestel Verlag, 1954, 1967, 1978, 1984, 1992.

Day, William E. *Blue Book of Art Values*. Third Edition. Paducah, KY: Collector Books, 1979.

Dyboski, Roman. *Outlines of Polish History*. London: George Allen & Unwin, Ltd. Revised edition, 1931.

Encyclopedia Britannica. Vol. 18. Chicago: William Benton, 1970.

Fayard, Artheme (ed.). *Souvernirs De Mme. Louise Elisabeth Vigee-LeBrun*. Paris: F. Funch-Bretana.

Gaston, Mary Frank. *The Collector's Encyclopedia of Limoges Porcelain*. Paducah, KY: Collector Books, 1980.

_____. *The Collector's Encyclopedia of R.S. Prussia*. Paducah, KY: Collector Books, 1982.

_____. "Rare R.S. (Schlegelmilch) Marks." *Schroeder's Insider*, December, 1983.

_____. "More Schlegelmilch Marks!" *Schroeder's Insider*, October, 1984.

_____. *The Collector's Encylopedia of R.S. Prussia*, Second Series. Paducah, KY: Collector Books, 1986.

_____. "Schlegelmilch China: Ambiguous, Scarce, and New Marks." Presentation at the annual meeting of the International Association of R.S.Prussia Collectors, Inc., August, 1991.

Graul, Richard and Albrecht Kurzwelly. *Alt Thuringer Porzellan*, 1909.

Haggar, Reginald G. *The Concise Encyclopedia of Continental Pottery and Porcelain*. New York: Hawthorne Books, Inc., 1960.

Hall, James. *Dictionary of Subjects and Symbols in Art*. Revised edition. New York: Harper & Row, 1979.

Hammon, Dorothy. *Confusing Collectibles*. Des Moines, Iowa: Wallace Homestead, 1969.

Hartwich, Bernd. *The History of the Suhl Porcelain Factories 1861-1937*. Tasked by the Technical School for Museum Caretakers. Leipzieg & Weapons Museum, Suhl, Germany, 1984. (Translation by R.H. Capers.)

Hayden, C. Chumley. *Why R.S. Prussia?* Springfield, OR: C. Chumley Hayden, 1970.

Heimatkalender des Kreifes Falkenberg (Hometown Almanac for the County of Falkenberg), 1927. (Translation by R. H. Capers.)

Honey, W.B. *German Porcelain*. London: Faber and Faber, MCMXLVII.

Hymanson, Albert M. *A Dictionary of Universal Biography of all Ages and of all People*. Second Edition. New York: E.P. Dutton & Co., Inc. 1951.

"Wilhelm Kahlert." Obituary in *Grottkain-Falkenberger Heimatblat*, Nr. 24, 1967. (Translation by R.H. Capers.)

Klingenbrunn, Marietta. *Deutsche Porzellanmarken von 1708 bis heute*. Augsburg, Germany: Battenburg Verlag, 1990.

Kovel, Ralph and Terry. *Kovel's New Dictionary of Marks*. New York: Crown Publications, Inc., 1986.

Kraemer, Ekkehard. *Sächsisch-thüringisches Manufakturporzellan*, 1985.

LaRousse Encyclopedia of World Geography. New York: Odyssey Press. Adapted form Geogaphie Universelle Larousse, Western Publishing Co., 1965.

Lehner, Lois. *Complete Book of American Kitchen and Dinnerware*. Des Moines: Wallace-Homestead, 1980.

_____ *Lehner's Encyclopedia of U.S. Marks on Pottery, Porcelain & Clay*. Paducah, KY: Collector Books, 1988.

Lehr, Margaret Marshall and Margaret Pattie Follet. *A Scrapbook About Old China*. Moorhead, MN: Follett Studios, 1964.

Leistikow-Duchardt, Annelore. *Die Entwicklung eines neuen Stiles im Porzellan*. Heidelberg: Carl Winter Universitatsverlag, 1957.

Lewis, C.T. Courtney. *The Picture Printer of the Ninteenth Century: George Baxter*. London: Sampson Law, Marsten & Co., Ltd. 1911.

Lucas, E.V. *Chardin and Vigee-Lebrun*. London: Methuen & Co., Ltd, .n.d.

McCaslin, Mary. "A Visit to Tillowitz, Poland – A Lot of Surprises." *R.S. Prussia* (Number 18, July 1992): 5-7.

McCaslin, Mary and Robert. "R.S. Prussia Club Restores Schlegelmilch Grave Site." *Antique Week* (July 27, 1992): 12 and 23.

McCaslin, Robert. "Answers From the Past." *R.S.Prussia* (Number 18, July 1992): 8.

Marple, Lee. "Hidden Images." Presentation at the annual meeting of the International Association of R.S. Prussia Collectors, Inc., August, 1991.

Meyers Grosses Konversations-Lexikon. Sixth Edition. Vol 17. Leipzig and Vienna: Biogaphisches Institut, 1907.

Mountfield, David. *The Antique Collectors' Illustrated Dictionary*. London, Hamlyn, 1974.

Muehsam, Gerd (ed.). *French Painters and Paintings from the Fourteenth Century to Post Impressionism*. New York: Fredrich Ungar Publishing Co., 1970.

Norman, Colleen and Rose Greider. "Identification of Unmarked Pieces." Presentation at the annual meeting of the International Association of R.S. Prussia Collectors, Inc., August, 1991.

Norman, Geraldine. *Nineteenth-Century Painters and Painting: A Dictionary*. Thames and Hudson, 1977.

Pattloch, Franz. "Erinnerung an Tillowitz/Oberichelian" [Memories of Tillowitz, Upper Silesia]. No date or source for periodical; post World War II refugee publication. (Translated by R. H. Capers.)

Penkala, Maria. *European Porcelain: A Handbook for the Collector*. Second Edition. Rutland, VT: Charles E. Tuttle, 1968.

Poche, Emanuel. *Porcelain Marks of the World*. New York: Arco Publishing Co., Inc., 1974.

Porcelit Tulowicki [Stoneware from Tulowice]. Monograph of the "Tillowice" Porcelit Plant as presented by the Exhibition Office, Opole, June-July 1984. (Translated by Roman Zawada.)

"Porzellan kommt aus OS" [Porcelain Comes out of Upper Silesia]. *Breslauer Neweste Nachrichten* (April 10, 1938). (Translated by R.H. Capers.)

Röntgen, Robert E. *Marks on German, Bohemian and Austrain Porcelain: 1710 to the Present*. Exton, PA: Schiffer Publishing Co., 1981.

Rose, William John. *The Drama of Upper Silesia*. Brattleboro, VT: Stephen Daye Press, 1935.

Schlegelmilch, Clifford J. *Handbook of Erdmann and Reinhold Schlegelmilch, Prussia-Germany and Oscar Schlegelmilch, Germany*. Third Edition, 1973.

Sorenson, Don C. *My Collection R.S. Prussia*, 1979.

Stryienski, Casimir (ed.) *Memoirs of the Countess Potocka*. New York Doubleday & McClure Co., 1901.

Terrell, George W., Jr. *Collecting R.S. Prussia: Identification and Values*. Florence, AL: Books Americana, 1982.

Thalheim, Karl G. and A. Hillen Ziegfeld (eds.). *Der deutsche Osten. Seine Geschichte, sein Wesen und seine Aufgabe*. Berlin: Propylaen, 1936.

The Antique Trader Price Guide to Antiques. Dubuque, IA: Babka Publishing Company, Inc., Summer 1979, Volume X, No.2, Issue No. 32.

The Ceramist. Vol. 3 (Winter Quarter), 1923.

The International Geographic Encyclopedia and Atlas. Boston: Houghton Mifflin Company, 1979.

The World Book Atlas. Field Enterprises Educational Corporation, 1973.

Thorne, J.O. (ed.). *Chambers Biographical Dictionary*. Revised edition. New York: St. Martin's Press, 1969.

Treharne, R.F. and Harold Fullard (eds.). *Muir's Historical Atlas Medieval and Modern*. Tenth Edition. New York: Barnes and Noble, Inc., 1964.

Wandycz, Piotr S. *The Lands of Paritioned Poland, 1795-1918*. Seattle: University of Washington Press, 1923.

Warzecha, Richard. "Ein Besuch in der Tillowitzer Porzellanfabrik" [A Visit to the Tillowitz Porcelain Factory], circa 1953. Publication source unknown. (Translated by R. H. Capers.)

Webster's Biographical Dictionary. Springfield, MA: G. and C. Merriam Company, 1976.

Webster's New Geographical Dictionary. Springfield, MA; G. and C. Merriam Company, 1972.

Weis, Gustav. *Ullstein Porzellanbuch*. Frankfurt, Berlin, Wein: Verlag Ullstein Gimblt, 1975. First Edition, 1964.

Wenke, George. "Tillowitzer Porzellaneschichte." *Unser Oberschlesien* (August 22, 1984). (Translated by R. H. Capers.)

Zühlsdorff, Dieter. *Marken Exikon – Porzellan und Keramik Report 1885-1935*. Stuttgart: Arnoldsche, 1988.

R.S. Prussia Mold Identification Chart
and Popular Names

Please note that some examples of RSP Molds shown in R.S. Prussia Series I and II are not repeated in this book. Those Molds and their numbers can be found in those editions. Some new molds, which are very similar to, but not identical with, other molds have been assigned mold numbers with "a, b, c" added to the number. Some new molds are described briefly in their first caption to highlight distinguishing characteristics which may not be obvious in the photograph.

Category 1 – Flat or Round Objects			
Mold Numbers	Plate Numbers	Type of Mold	General Characteristics
1-50	1-81	Popular Named Molds (Iris, etc.)	A particular feature in the body or the border of the mold suggests an obvious mold name.
51-75	82-86	Floral Border Molds	The border of the mold is composed of floral designs usually separated by other shapes such as scallops or points. The floral designs are not always easy to see at first glance.
76-150	87-141	Unusual Body Shape	The body of the mold is composed of blown out sections usually in the form of dome or star shapes.
151-180	142-150	Pointed Border Molds	The overall border design is pointed. There may be notched identations between the points. Such molds must be easily distinguishable from scalloped molds and have no rounded sides.
181-200	151-155	Rounded Scalloped Border	Border has rounded scallop sections of equal size. The sections may be beaded or fluted.
201-250	156-170	Seim-Round Scalloped Border	The scallop sections are not perfectly round. There may be a slight indentation or some other configuration between the scallops. The edges of the scallops can be smooth, beaded, or fluted.
251-275	171-186	Crimped Scalloped Border	Scallop sections are pinched or indented.
276-299	187-192	Wavy Scalloped Border	The scallop sections resembles a wavy line with a slight rounded center and shallow indentations on each side. The wavy sections may be separated by other small configurations such as scroll designs or points.
300-325	193-209	Elongated Scalloped Border	The scallop sections are long rather than round. The center of the section has either a slight indentation or a sharp rounded point. The elongated scallops may be separated by other small configurations.
326-400	210-229	Irregular Scalloped Borders	Borders are composed of more than one of the above kind of scallops or some other configuration such as a point or scroll design. These molds are usually quite elaborate.
401-425	230-232	Scrolled Borders	Border is composed of ornate, curving scallop designs not only on the border but extending into the body of the object.
426-450	233-244	Smooth Borders	Border is completely smooth. The overall shape of the object may vary: round, oval, or rectangular.

Category 2 – Vertical or Tall Objects			
Mold Numbers	Plate Numbers	Type of Mold	General Characteristics
451-500	245-262;323	Smooth Bases	Base of object is perfectly level or flat on the bottom.
501-575	263-322; 324-363	Flat Scalloped Base	The border of the base of the object is scalloped, but there is no elevation.
576-600	364-375	Elevated Scalloped Base	The base of the object has a scallop border composed of equal or varied sized scallops. Indentations between the scallops elevate the object slightly.
601-625	376-391	Pedestal Foot	Objects may have a long or a short pedestal base. Long pedestals have a stem section between the base and body; short pedestals have no stem section. The bases of the pedestals may be round, square, smooth, or scalloped.
626-700	392-472	Molded Feet	Feet for the object are shaped as part of the body mold.
701-725	473-487	Applied Feet	Definite feet are applied to the base of the object.

Category 3 – Accessory Items		
Mold Numbers	Plate Numbers	Type of Mold
726-775	488-489	Hatpin Holders
776-800	490-493	Muffineers/Talcum Shakers
801-825	494-504	Hair Receivers
826-850	505-516	Boxes: Match, Pin, Powder
851-855	517	Candle Holders
856-860	– –	Letter Holders

Category 4 – Ferners and Vases		
Mold Numbers	Plate Numbers	Type of Mold
876-899	518-522	Ferners
900-950	524-583	Vases/Ewers/Urns

Mold Numbers and Popular Names
(Gaston Mold Numbers may be found variously in either the First, Second, or Third Series)

Gaston Mold Number	Popular Name	Gaston Mold Number	Popular Name
1, 583	Acorn	502	Morning Glory
632	Ball Foot		Nut (see Acorn)
32, 32a, 32b	Berry	586	Open Base
33	Bleeding Heart	528, also 802	Pagoda
504, 813	Bow Tie	15	Pentagon
	Cabbage (see Lettuce)	36, 649; also 255, 256	Pie Crust
28, 28a, 519, 520, 526; also 55, 402	Carnation or Poppy	951; also 952	Pillow
	Circle (see Madallion)	16, 465, 658, 836	Plume
261	Corduroy	81, 82, 611, 643	Point and Clover
	Daisy (see Lily)	91	Point and Flower
548	Daisy and Scroll	92	Popcorn
841	Egg Basket or Carton	17	Puff
601	Egg on Pedestal	657	Raspberry
	Feather (see Plume)	451, 472, 545, 634	Reversed Swirl
207, 642	Flame and Jewel	18, 522, 645, 817, 835, 932, 936, 963; also 333	Ribbon and Jewel
646	Fleur and Jewel	259, 536, 815	Ripple
9, 609, 929; also 214	Fleur-de-lys	300	Rope Edge
527	Flower Form		Ruffle (see Stippled Floral)
2, 2a, 2b, 2c	Grape	98	Sawtooth
3	Heart	508, 540, 540a, 729	Scallop
577	Hexagon	278, 501	Scallop and Fan
34	Honey Comb	19	Sea Creature
7, 8, 466, 641, 806	Icicle	20	Shell
25, 25a, 25b, 518, 628	Iris	37, 37a	Shield
257	Ivy and Icicle	78	Six Medallion
	Jewel (see Ribbon and Jewel)	21	Spoonholder
10, 10a through 10i	Leaf	22	Square and Jewel
627, 627a, 627b	Leaf Base	23, 525, 826	Stippled Floral
12, 12a, 12b	Lettuce	38, 482	Strawberry
29, 30, 517	Lily	31, 463, 553, 626	Sunflower
473	Lily of the Valley	155, 582, 633	Swag and Tassel
53, 53a	Lily Pad	39	Tear Drop
35, 35a, 35b	Locket	40, 811, 839	Tulip and Ribbon
13	Maize	90	Violet
14, 14a, 631	Medallion	24	Wheat Fleur-de-lys

Creative Artists' Signatures

These four photographs illustrate details of R.S. Prussia floral transfers. Signatures are shown of the artisans who either designed the mold or the art work for the original transfer. Kolb, Klett, and Rein were mold makers; Happ was a design painter.

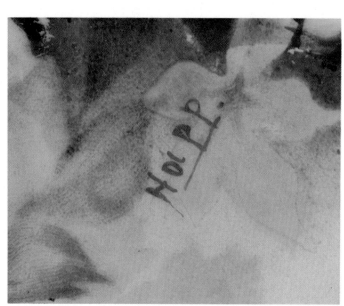

Reinhold Schlegelmilch Family Tree*

(Underscored names indicate line of family ownership of RS factory)

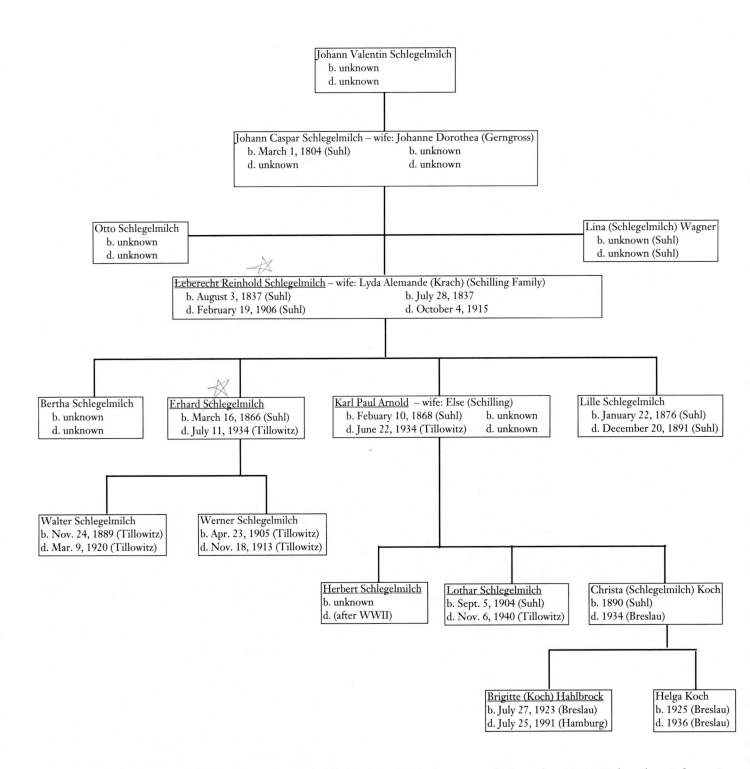

*The Reinhold Schlegelmilch Family Tree was compiled by Mr. R. H. Capers as of November 17, 1992, based on information in the Hartwich (1984) manuscript, available death notices, actual grave sites, church records, and interviews with Herr Dr. Soppa and Herr Dr. Hahlbrock. Minor changes or revisions may be necessary if new information becomes available.

Death Notices For Reinhold Schlegelmilch

These notices were published in local newspapers at the time. The first notice was placed by Reinhold Schlegelmilch's family with the individual names listed: Lyda Schlegelmilch (wife); Lina Wagner (neé Schlegelmilch, probably Reinhold's sister); Otto Schlegelmilch (brother); Erhard Schlegelmilch (oldest son); Bertha Schlegelmilch (daughter, based on ranking); Oscar Schlegelmilch (son-in-law, Bertha's husband and possibly a descendant of Erdmann Schlegelmilch; to date, this appears to be the only known tie between the Erdmann Schlegelmilch and Reinhold Schlegelmilch families).

The second announcement was placed by the factory officials and employees of the Reinhold Schlegelmilch Factories in Suhl and Tillowitz.

The third notice was placed by the Suhl Municipal Council. It states that Reinhold Schlegelmilch was a Senator of the Municipal Council, had received an honorary Knighthood, and had served for twenty-seven years as a member of the Council and as its Chairman.

Copies of the death notices and translations are provided by Mr. R. H. Capers.

Es hat dem Herrn gefallen, meinen lieben Mann, unseren teueren Vater und Schwiegervater,

den Königlichen Kommerzienrat

Herrn Reinhold Schlegelmilch

heute Morgen aus arbeitsreichem Leben nach kurzer Krankheit im 69. Lebensjahr abzurufen.

Suhl, 19. Februar 1906.

In tiefer Trauer

Frau Kommerzienrat Lyda Schlegelmilch } Suhl.
Frau Lina Wagner, geb. Schlegelmilch }
Otto Schlegelmilch u. Frau, Falkenberg O.-S.
Erhard Schlegelmilch u. Frau, Tillowitz O.-S.
Arnold Schlegelmilch u. Frau, Suhl
Frau Bertha Schlegelmilch } Langewiesen.
Oscar Schlegelmilch }

Einem Wunsch des Verstorbenen nachkommend, bitten wir, Kranzspenden zu unterlassen.

Beerdigung Donnerstag Vormittag 11 Uhr vom Trauerhause.

Nachruf.

Nach kurzer Krankheit endete gestern früh ein sanfter Tod das arbeitsreiche Leben unseres hochverehrten Senior-Chefs, des

Fabrikbesitzers und Königlichen Kommerzienrates

Herrn Reinhold Schlegelmilch

in Suhl.

Stets unermüdlich im Wirken und Schaffen, ausgezeichnet durch seltenen Rechtlichkeitssinn und Herzensgüte, betrauern wir in dem Entschlafenen einen für das Wohl seiner Beamten und Arbeiter treu sorgenden Prinzipal, dessen Andenken wir alle Zeit in Ehren halten werden.

Suhl und Tillowitz, den 20. Februar 1906

Die Beamten- und Arbeiterpersonale der Firma
Reinhold Schlegelmilch.

In der Nacht vom 18. zum 19. d. Mts. verschied plötzlich nach kurzem Krankenlager unser hochverehrtes und verdientes Mitglied

der Königliche Kommerzienrat und Senator

Reinhold Schlegelmilch

Ritter pp.

Ueber 27 Jahre hat der Verblichene im Magistratskollegium gewirkt, nachdem er vorher bereits seit dem Jahre 1870 als Stadtverordneter und seit dem Jahre 1875 als Vorsteher der Versammlung der Stadtvertretung angehört hat.

In dieser langen Zeit hat er unermüdlich seine reichen Kenntnisse und sein warmes Herz in den Dienst der Stadt gestellt, und manche wertvolle Errungenschaft wie die Wasserleitung und das städtische Krankenhaus verdankt nicht zum wenigsten seiner rastlosen Tätigkeit ihr Entstehen.

Selbstgewöhnt, die größten Anforderungen an sich zu stellen, verband er mit einer unvergleichlichen Selbstlosigkeit eine Milde und Herzensgüte, die allen, die mit ihm in nähere Beziehungen traten, das Herz erwärmte.

Uns, denen er ein stets hilfsbereiter Freund und Kollege war, wird sein Andenken unvergeßlich bleiben.

Suhl, den 19. Februar 1906.

Das Magistratskollegium.

Dr. Hagemeister. Janssen. Alb. Schilling. Oskar Jung. Haenel.
Aug. Hartung. R. Wilh. Rober.

R.S. Tillowitz Factory

Some views of the Reinhold Schlegelmilch Factory in Tillowitz

RST Factory

View of Factory from the railroad yard; the five kilns can be seen.

Original Warehouse

Inner Courtyard of Factory

One of the original five kilns

Drying Room above kilns

Original Admistration Building

Close-up view of Entrance to Administration Building (Note the 1904 date which is later than when the factory buildings were built.)

Photographs and information provided by Mr. R. H. Capers.

Schlegelmilch Homes

Erhard Schlegelmilch's home in Tillowitz is referred to as the "old" villa, because it was built before Erhard's brother, Arnold, moved from Suhl to Tillowitz. Arnold's home became known as the "new" villa.

A porcelain chandelier hanging in the stairwell at one end of the grand hallway in the old villa. This chandelier is quite noteworthy and has been the subject of several articles. It is considered to be a museum piece. The chandelier is made of all white porcelain. The molds for it were designed by the factory's chief mold maker, Wilhelm Kahlert, based on a design by the Berlin sculptor, Frey. It hangs by hollow porcelain links, approximately 15 feet from the ceiling. The crown of the chandelier is about three feet in diameter. The stained glass windows in the background are also attributed to designs by Frey. The date "1912" appears on windows in an upstairs bathroom.

Exterior view of Erhard's home, the "old" villa, built ca. 1912.

Wall relief work of hand plaster over main entrance in entry hall of the old villa.

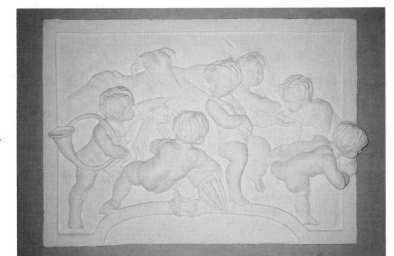

Relief work on wall of children's room in old villa.

Fireplace in Entry Hall.

Formal Dining Room in the old villa.

Front Entrance to Arnold's home, the new villa, probably built after World War I.

Back view of the new villa.

Side view of the new villa.

Photographs and information provided by Mr. R. H. Capers.

Descendants' Burial Sites

The following photographs show the former Lutheran Church (now Catholic) in Tillowitz which was built by the Schlegelmilchs in 1912. The grave yard is behind the church through the arched entrance to the left of the tower. The Schlegelmilch family plot was located on April 28, 1992, by Mr. R. H. Capers and Mary and Bob McCaslin. The photographs are from their collections.

Tillowitz Lutheran Church

Schlegelmilch Family Marker, 1.72 cm high, 75.5 cm wide (at arms); base, 129cm.

The following five photos are of the individual grave markers for Erhard, Arnold, Walter, Lothar, and Werner. Pictures were taken by the McCaslins on April 28, 1992, when the graves were located.

This photo was taken by Mr. Capers in November, 1992, after the site had been restored through the efforts of Mr. Capers and the McCaslins with funds contributed by the International Association of R.S. Prussia Collectors, Inc.

Current Successor to the Reinhold Schlegelmilch Tillowitz Factory

The name of the current porcelain factory in Tillowitz which is the successor to the Reinhold Schlegelmilch Factory is **Zaklady Porcelitu Stolowego**.

The "P.T." Wreath Mark is used by the factory on its wares. A mosaic of the mark is shown.

View of Factory

Mold Room

Showcases of Current Production

Showcases of Current Production

Photographs and information provided by Mr. R. H. Capers.

Photographs from the 1992 Exhibit Celebrating Schlegelmilch Porcelain

On November 8, 1992 an exhibit of porcelain manufactured by the E.S., R.S., & C.S. Factories was opened in Suhl. Over 300 examples were displayed. The majority of those were donated by the townspeople. Herr Eduard Hoffmann, a porcelain painter and mold maker for the E.S. Factory from 1927 to 1935 attended the event. Pieces shown here are from the Exhibit which Mr. and Mrs. R. H. Capers attended. Photographs are theirs from the exhibit.

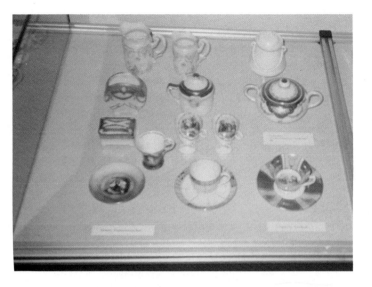

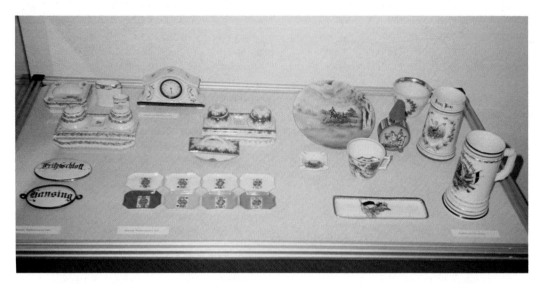
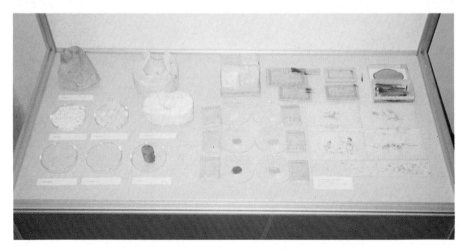

These are samples of Herr Eduard Hoffmann's tools of trade.

Index to R.S. Prussia Floral Decoration

One hundred floral transfers found on R.S. Prussia marked china have been assigned a Floral Identification number for this edition. The numbers include some of the popular named floral patterns such as "Reflecting Water Lilies," "Roses and Snowballs," "Hanging Basket," and so forth. These various popular named patterns are described by number and name in the captions of the photographs. The other floral patterns are described by number with a brief description of the design. The description is not always included in the caption, however. Readers may refer to this index to find the description of the numbered pattern if necessary. A list of the RSP Floral Identification numbers (FD#) and their descriptions are provided here. Examples of those specific floral transfers shown in the photographs are listed by Plate number.

To describe the floral patterns, I have used only the chief characteristics of the paricular design. The number generally refers to the primary pattern on the piece. Sometimes two floral transfers may be found on the same piece, and, thus, the example will have more then one FD#. The large center floral decorations usually do have other floral designs scattered randomly around the inner and outer borders. These may differ from the central pattern, but such designs are not identified by FD# unless the design is one of the 100 transfers used for this Identification System.

I also have not assigned numbers to most of the small floral patterns such as small garlands, single blooms, and small clusters of flowers. The numbers are basically restricted to the larger patterns. Some of the names used to describe the floral designs may differ among collectors from those I use here. Some of the flowers are not easily distinguishable. Roses may look like poppies and vice versa. Lilacs, pansies, clematis, and so forth are other floral shapes which might be confusing. The colors may vary for the patterns, either by design, or through the lighting used for the photograph. Pink, yellow, white, and orange as well as other colors may appear either darker or lighter than they actually are. Thus, a red may appear as dark pink, or a pale yellow may seem to be white. The configuration of the floral design is more important in determining a specific pattern than the color of the flowers.

The floral patterns found on R.S. Prussia china appear to be endless, but after studying hundreds of examples, it is evident that the number of primary designs are probably in the low hundreds rather than thousands. The placement of the embellishments around the central patterns makes it appear as though there are more patterns than there actually are. The one hundred designs identified here are certainly not all of the primary floral patterns. From the photographs, which are from a random sample, it is apparent that many pieces and molds have the same floral pattern. A few of the FD numbers are listed with an "a" or "b." These letters indicate that the pattern is either similar to the one with the whole number, or that it is a part of that transfer.

RSP FD#	Description of Pattern	Examples (by Plate Number)
1	three full light pink roses and one dark pink rose	1, 90, 313
2	multi-colored roses with a white rose on a hair-pin bent stem	2, 42, 83, 108, 373, 412, 436
3	one red rose and one white rose	3, 34, 59, 107, 182, 194, 316, 330, 411, 425, 427, 509, 524, 548, 551
4	pink and white roses with one pink rose offshoot	6, 28, 31
5	two large pink roses with two rose offshoots	40, 296, 338
5a	the two large roses from FD5	96, 125, 327, 379
6	pink poppies and Lily of the Valley	8, 11, 23, 27, 329, 371, 400, 463
7	two open bloom pink roses and two smaller blooms	44, 48, 63, 368, 377, 378, 417, 435, 486, 538
8	multi-colored roses	13, 46, 47, 51, 82, 88, 106, 129, 165, 382, 383, 384, 397, 442
9	four large pink poppies with one closed poppy	50, 89, 109, 554, 557, 570
10	a branch with two pink roses and one white rose	41

RSP FD#	Description of Pattern	Examples (by Plate Number)
11	large yellow roses with one white rose	113, 115
11a	partial rose design from FD11	173
12	white roses with one orange bloom (colors may vary)	5, 187, 191, 251, 258
13	two orange roses and one pink rose	17, 133
13a	two pink roses and one yellow rose (similar to FD13)	18
14	pink roses with one orange rose and a cluster of white daisies at base of branch	58, 94, 162, 167, 195, 230
15	multi-colored roses with a small daisy cluster	67, 91, 93, 100, 150, 159
16	multi-colored poppies (colors may vary)	53, 68, 81, 85, 198, 213, 413
17	large white poppies with multi-colored poppies	79, 160, 229, 272
18	one white open poppy and one closed orange poppy	15, 142, 163, 196, 278, 348, 386, 416, 491, 590
18a	a large white petaled flower (similar to one in FD18)	416
19	a yellow, a white, and two pink roses	38, 476
20	a pink and a yellow open bloom rose with one small pink bud	77, 127, 304, 310, 315, 471
20a	the yellow rose from FD20	128
21	multi-colored mums and other flowers	4
22	clusters of small multi-colored flowers	37, 275, 276
23	white flower with a yellow center, yellow blossoms, and a yellow rose offshoot	20, 228, 588
23a	variation of FD23	228
24	pink-peach colored roses and a bud	21, 257
25	Magnolias	52, 303, 333, 352, 353, 428, 438, 440, 563, 564
25a	FD25 with one closed flower at top	61, 62, 84
26	dark pink and light pink lilies	54, 57, 63, 90, 314, 437, 452
27	one large pink rose with one pink bud	59
28	dark pink and light pink roses	60, 92
29	spray of pink lilies	76
30	a pink rose with a small white flower	92, 99, 381
30a	a pink rose with a small white flower and daisies	137
31	Roses and snowballs	97, 98, 114, 231, 253, 451
31a	variation of FD31 with flowers in a glass bowl	252, 380, 431, 432
32	a large light pink rose and a smaller white rose	242, 521
33	pink poppies and a snowball	101, 116, 181, 429
34	seven scattered flowers	104
35	one light pink and two dark pink roses	112

RSP FD#	Description of Pattern	Examples (by Plate Number)
36	Reflecting Poppies and Daisies	24, 118, 203, 403, 404, 488
37	one large dark pink rose, one white rose, and a shaggy pink blossom and bud	119, 183
38	Reflecting Water Lilies	32, 35, 201, 419, 506
39	lilac clematis	75, 126, 300, 311, 456, 470, 505, 571, 580
40	bouquet of light and dark pink carnations	130, 131, 517
41	cluster of small lilac flowers	136, 512
42	two large pale pink roses with three buds	139
43	light and dark pink roses with two yellow roses and one light pink offshoot	80
44	Hanging Basket	12, 140, 147, 211, 346, 367, 420, 510, 550
45	green-brown leaves with grain head	144
46	one pink rose with small white leaves	134
47	two white Lilies with Dogwood	153, 326, 336, 344
48	a white water liliy and a yellow rose; also appears with scattered flowers (FD34)	104, 156
49	Surreal Dogwood	159, 249, 337
49a	Surreal Dogwood with gold enamelled stems	36, 175, 176, 189, 209, 245, 248, 267, 501
49b	FD49 in various colors	264, 270
50	a large full bloom dark pink rose	171
51	white bonnet shaped flowers with yellow pods	172
52	a red rose, a pink rose, and a white rose with red center	558, 575
53	dark pink, light pink, and yellow roses	178, 262, 265, 266, 394
54	bouquet of yellow tinted lilies and a bud	214
55	cluster of three roses in shades of pink	182, 232
56	Daffodils	185
57	a large dark pink rose and bud with a pale pink rose	224
58	large brown and green leaves with a cluster of yellow seed pods	239
59	spray of small white flowers	234, 236
60	one large white rose and one large pink rose	237, 238
61	two large pink roses with a white leaf	222
62	spray of small light and dark pink roses	215, 335, 423
63	small yellow and white flowers with a lilac shadow	219
64	two pale yellow roses with one offshoot	235

RSP FD#	Description of Pattern	Examples (by Plate Number)
65	two large pink roses on long stems with green leaves	210
66	large green leaves on vine with small white flowers	205, 254
67	cluster of white flowers with offshoots of a pair of orange and pink blooms	208
68	two white flowers with one orange flower outlined in gold	207
69	single daisy with laurel chain	206
70	large pink roses and a bud	197
71	one large white spider mum, one dark pink open rose, and a dark pink rose offshoot	135, 226
72	one light pink and one dark pink rose with two small buds and two blooms extending from center	188
73	a pink and a white tulip	174, 246, 325
74	a large cluster of multi-colored roses and green leaves on a branch	148
75	three pink roses with green leaves	149
76	spray of shaggy pink roses	36, 168
77	white blossoms with a lavender tint	155, 268
78	a large white and a large pink open petal blossom with a closed white bloom at top and a small pink flower at bottom	516
79	Calla Lily	250, 287, 585
80	cluster of large open pink-orange blooms	255, 341
81	white poppies with a pink tint	286, 366
82	two large white blossoms with yellow centers	288
83	large open bloom white flowers	289
84	cluster of purple and white flowers	324
85	Lily of the Valley	260, 465, 473, 474, 493
86	a pink rose spray with an offshoot of two entwined buds and green leaves	36, 274, 277, 340, 458-460; 468, 482
86a	spray of three pink roses and one offshoot	457
86b	spray of large pink roses with an offshoot of three blooms with green leaves	478
87	evergreen branch	294
88	cluster of white roses	241, 323
89	cluster of pink and white tulips	292
90	Sitting Basket	29, 273, 399
91	spray of pink flowers with one large white flower	339, 343, 519
92	cluster of purple and small white flowers	363, 913
93	large pink flowers with two buds	415

RSP FD#	Description of Pattern	Examples (by Plate Number)
94	cluster of red and white roses	418
95	Canterbury Bells (color may vary)	454, 455
96	pink and white spider mums	461
97	Dogwood and Pine	see G2, Plate 260
98	one light pink and two dark pink roses with a dark pink rose offshoot	305
98a	same transfer as FD98, except offshoot is a bud rather than a full rose	305
99	Spray of pink and white carnations	479
100	a dark pink and a light pink rose with a light pink rose offshoot	480

Index to R.S. Prussia Decoration Themes

Animal:
    Lions – 542, 549
    Tigers – 217, 331
Barnyard Animals – 199, 529
Birds:
    Bird of Paradise – 574
    Blue Bird, see Swallows
    Ducks – 199
        Black Duck – 370, 507
        Indian Runner Duck – 199
    Hummingbirds – 334, 543, 547
    Ostrich – 531
    Quail – 158
    Parrots – 364
    Peacocks – 530
    Pheasants – 25, 199, 202, 359, 534
    Snow Bird – 9, 26, 138, 406, 422
    Snow Geese – 157
    Swallows – 30, 202, 360, 369, 376, 390, 401, 489, 537
    Swans in Lake – 7, 23, 30, 118, 145, 161, 202, 360, 365, 400, 405, 421, 490, 520, 540, 552, 553, 594
        with Evergreens – 169, 414, 541
        with Gazebo – 216
        with Terrace – 453
    Turkeys – 199, 212
Figural:
    The Cage – 218, 581
    Diana The Huntress – 576
    Dice Throwers – 102, 120, 434, 446, 565, 583
    Flora (Reclining Lady) – 22, 103, 227, 559, 577
    Melon Eaters – 447, 525, 545, 554, 567
        Single Melon Eater – 120, 433, 434, 446-449, 533, 582
    Nightwatch Figures – 536
    Victorian Vignettes
        Courting Couple – 532

    Lady Feeding Chickens – 103
    Lady with Dog – 103
    Lady Watering Flowers – 103
Fruit:
    I (Mixed Fruit) – 39, 166, 186, 372
    II (Grapes, Apples, Cherries) – 141
    III (three Pears) – 152
    IV (Peach, Pear, Strawberry, Plum) – 154
    V (Pears and Grapes) – 180, 355
    VI (Sliced Orange) – 462
Portraits:
    Countess Potocka – 27, 28, 69, 299, 580
    Flossie – 179, 485
    Four Seasons:
        Fall (Autumn) – 16, 64, 65, 72, 107, 398
        Spring – 45, 66, 87, 107, 221, 396, 441, 561, 568
        Summer – 43, 49, 107, 318, 556
        Winter – 107, 220, 439, 443, 469, 523, 560, 562, 569
    Gibson Girls – 143, 163
    Madame LeBrun
        I (ribbon in hair) – 27, 28, 70, 71, 295, 298, 404, 472, 572
        II (with cap) – 27, 74, 297, 299, 362, 578
    Madame Récamier – 27, 28, 73, 295, 299, 309, 472, 571, 579
    Miscellaneous – 225, 395
Scenic
    Castle (or church) – 110, 121-123, 308, 345, 358, 407, 408, 444, 546
    Cottage – 111, 122, 307, 409, 410, 430, 526, 527, 566
    Masted Schooner – 332, 426
    Mill – 44, 122, 124, 193, 408, 489, 528, 537, 539, 555
    Old Man in the Mountain – 10, 26, 117, 184, 200, 402, 540, 552
    Sheeperder I – 26, 390
    Three Scenes – 202

Index to R.S. Prussia Objects
(By Plate Numbers)

Value Guide
(Identified by Plate Numbers)

# 1.................$300.00 - 350.00	# 55.................$450.00 - 550.00	# 108.................$400.00 - 500.00
# 2.................$300.00 - 350.00	# 56.................$400.00 - 500.00	# 109.................$225.00 - 275.00
# 3.................$325.00 - 375.00	# 57.................$350.00 - 450.00	# 110.................$600.00 - 700.00
# 4.................$350.00 - 400.00	# 58.................$600.00 - 700.00	# 111.................$400.00 - 500.00
# 5.................$225.00 - 275.00	# 59.................$140.00 - 180.00	# 112.................$250.00 - 300.00
# 6.................$150.00 - 175.00	# 60...................$50.00 - 60.00	# 113.................$350.00 - 400.00
# 7.................$500.00 - 600.00	# 61.................$600.00 - 700.00	# 114.................$350.00 - 450.00
# 8.................$175.00 - 225.00	# 62.................$225.00 - 275.00	# 115.................$200.00 - 250.00
# 9.................$1400.00 - 1600.00	# 63.........(set) $800.00 - 1000.00	# 116.................$200.00 - 250.00
# 10.................$800.00 - 1000.00	# 64.................$2000.00 - 2200.00	# 117.................$500.00 - 600.00
# 11.................$500.00 - 600.00	# 65.................$1800.00 - 2000.00	# 118.................$400.00 - 500.00
# 12.................$200.00 - 250.00	# 66.................$1800.00 - 2000.00	# 119.................$250.00 - 300.00
# 13.................$225.00 - 275.00	# 67.................$275.00 - 325.00	# 120.................$1800.00 - 2000.00
# 14.................$200.00 - 250.00	# 68.................$350.00 - 400.00	# 121.................$600.00 - 700.00
# 15.................$250.00 - 300.00	# 69.................$1200.00 - 1400.00	# 122.........(set) $1000.00 - 1200.00
# 16.................$2200.00 - 2400.00	# 70.................$1400.00 - 1600.00	# 123.................$650.00 - 750.00
# 17.................$250.00 - 300.00	# 71.................$2200.00 - 2400.00	# 124.................$600.00 - 700.00
# 18.........(set) $800.00 - 1000.00	# 72.................$2000.00 - 2200.00	# 125.................$275.00 - 325.00
# 19.................$225.00 - 275.00	# 73.................$250.00 - 300.00	# 126.................$175.00 - 225.00
# 20.................$125.00 - 150.00	# 74.................$500.00 - 700.00	# 127.................$275.00 - 325.00
# 21.........(set) $200.00 - 250.00	# 75.................$225.00 - 275.00	# 128.................$200.00 - 250.00
# 22.................$800.00 - 1000.00	# 76.................$300.00 - 350.00	# 129.................$275.00 - 325.00
# 23.................$400.00 - 450.00	# 77.................$250.00 - 300.00	# 130.................$600.00 - 700.00
# 24.................$350.00 - 400.00	# 78.................$300.00 - 350.00	# 131.................$250.00 - 300.00
# 25.................$800.00 - 1000.00	# 79.................$275.00 - 325.00	# 132.................$125.00 - 150.00
# 26.................$1000.00 - 1200.00	# 80.................$300.00 - 350.00	# 133.................$150.00 - 175.00
# 27.................$1200.00 - 1400.00	# 81.................$300.00 - 350.00	# 134.................$250.00 - 300.00
# 28.................$1200.00 - 1400.00	# 82.................$225.00 - 275.00	# 135.................$500.00 - 600.00
# 29.................$175.00 - 225.00	# 83.................$250.00 - 300.00	# 136.................$225.00 - 275.00
# 30.................$250.00 - 300.00	# 84.................$175.00 - 200.00	# 137.................$250.00 - 300.00
# 31.................$200.00 - 250.00	# 85.................$400.00 - 500.00	# 138.................$1400.00 - 1600.00
# 32.................$200.00 - 250.00	# 86.................$140.00 - 160.00	# 139.........(set) $500.00 - 600.00
# 33.................$400.00 - 500.00	# 87.................$2000.00 - 2200.00	# 140.................$250.00 - 300.00
# 34.................$275.00 - 325.00	# 88.................$250.00 - 300.00	# 141.................$300.00 - 350.00
# 35.................$200.00 - 250.00	# 89.................$400.00 - 500.00	# 142.........(set) $500.00 - 600.00
# 36.................$250.00 - 300.00	# 90.................$275.00 - 325.00	# 143.................$1000.00 - 1200.00
# 37.................$175.00 - 225.00	# 91...................$50.00 - 60.00	# 144.................$200.00 - 250.00
# 38.................$300.00 - 400.00	# 92.........(Plate) $200.00 - 250.00	# 145.................$450.00 - 550.00
# 39.................$300.00 - 350.00	.................(Bowl) $225.00 - 275.00	# 146.................$175.00 - 225.00
# 40.................$275.00 - 325.00	# 93.................$200.00 - 250.00	# 147.................$150.00 - 200.00
# 41.................$300.00 - 400.00	# 94.................$250.00 - 300.00	# 148.................$300.00 - 350.00
# 42.................$350.00 - 450.00	# 95.................$250.00 - 300.00	# 149.................$175.00 - 225.00
# 43.................$1800.00 - 2000.00	# 96.................$200.00 - 250.00	# 150.................$450.00 - 550.00
# 44.................$600.00 - 700.00	# 97.................$350.00 - 450.00	# 151.................$300.00 - 350.00
# 45.................$1200.00 - 1400.00	# 98.................$300.00 - 350.00	# 152.................$250.00 - 300.00
# 46.................$400.00 - 500.00	# 99.................$200.00 - 250.00	# 153.................$250.00 - 300.00
# 47.................$250.00 - 300.00	# 100.................$275.00 - 325.00	# 154.................$300.00 - 350.00
# 48.................$300.00 - 350.00	# 101.................$275.00 - 325.00	# 155.........(set) $600.00 - 700.00
# 49.................$1400.00 - 1600.00	# 102.................$1800.00 - 2000.00	# 156.................$200.00 - 250.00
# 50.................$400.00 - 450.00	# 103.................$1400.00 - 1600.00	# 157.................$1400.00 - 1600.00
# 51.................$225.00 - 275.00	# 104.................$175.00 - 225.00	# 158.................$1400.00 - 1600.00
# 52.................$250.00 - 300.00	# 105.................$175.00 - 225.00	# 159.................$175.00 - 225.00
# 53.................$400.00 - 500.00	# 106.................$300.00 - 350.00	# 160.................$225.00 - 275.00
# 54.................$200.00 - 250.00	# 107.................$2000.00 - 2200.00	# 161.................$375.00 - 425.00

162 ....$175.00 - 225.00
163 ....$800.00 - 1000.00
164 ....$200.00 - 250.00
165 ....$250.00 - 300.00
166 ....$300.00 - 350.00
167 ....$175.00 - 225.00
168 ....$150.00 - 200.00
169 ....$450.00 - 550.00
170 ....$120.00 - 140.00
171 ....$125.00 - 150.00
172 ....$250.00 - 300.00
173 ....$150.00 - 175.00
174 ....$100.00 - 125.00
175 ....$80.00 - 100.00
176 ....$20.00 - 25.00
177 ....$140.00 - 160.00
178 ....$50.00 - 75.00
179 ....$300.00 - 400.00
180 ....$325.00 - 375.00
181 ....$200.00 - 250.00
182 ....$150.00 - 200.00
183 ....$250.00 - 300.00
184 ....$650.00 - 750.00
185 ....$70.00 - 90.00
186 ....$300.00 - 350.00
187 ....$200.00 - 250.00
188 ....$175.00 - 225.00
189 ....$40.00 - 50.00
190 ....$350.00 - 400.00
191 ....(set) $450.00 - 550.00
192 ....$125.00 - 175.00
193 ....$350.00 - 450.00
194 ....$325.00 - 375.00
195 ....$200.00 - 250.00
196 ....$200.00 - 250.00
197 ....$600.00 - 700.00
198 ....$225.00 - 275.00
199 ....$600.00 - 700.00
200 ....$600.00 - 700.00
201 ....$325.00 - 375.00
202 ....$400.00 - 500.00
203 ....$350.00 - 400.00
204 ....$250.00 - 300.00
205 ....$100.00 - 125.00
206 ....$120.00 - 140.00
207 ....$160.00 - 180.00
208 ....$80.00 - 100.00
209 ....$160.00 - 180.00
210 ....$60.00 - 75.00
211 ....$275.00 - 325.00
212 ....$600.00 - 700.00
213 ....$250.00 - 300.00
214 ....$300.00 - 350.00
215 ....$200.00 - 250.00
216 ....$400.00 - 500.00
217 ....$8000.00 - 10,000.00
218 ....$1000.00 - 1200.00
219 ....(set) $350.00 - 450.00

220 ....$1800.00 - 2000.00
221 ....$1800.00 - 2000.00
222 ....$150.00 - 175.00
223 ....$100.00 - 125.00
224 ....$400.00 - 500.00
225 ....$300.00 - 400.00
226 ....$175.00 - 225.00
227 ....$900.00 - 1100.00
228 ....(set) $400.00 - 500.00
229 ....$150.00 - 175.00
230 ....$225.00 - 275.00
231 ....$175.00 - 225.00
232 ....$80.00 - 100.00
233 ....$125.00 - 150.00
234 ....$150.00 - 175.00
235 ....$150.00 - 175.00
236 ....$125.00 - 150.00
237 ....$150.00 - 200.00
238 ....$150.00 - 200.00
239 ....$175.00 - 225.00
240 ....$140.00 - 180.00
241 ....$150.00 - 175.00
242 ....$250.00 - 300.00
243 ....$400.00 - 500.00
244 ....$450.00 - 550.00
245 ....(Pot) $250.00 - 300.00
........(Cup & Saucer, ea. set)$50.00 - 65.00
246 ....$300.00 - 350.00
247 ....(set) $250.00 - 350.00
248 ....$300.00 - 400.00
249 ....(Pot) $500.00 - 600.00
...(Cup & Saucer, ea. set) $100.00 - 125.00
250 ....$250.00 - 300.00
251 ....$250.00 - 300.00
252 ....$800.00 - 1000.00
253 ....$225.00 - 275.00
254 ....$250.00 - 300.00
255 ....$325.00 - 375.00
256 ....(set) $600.00 - 700.00
257 ....$100.00 - 125.00
258 ....(with lid) $125.00 - 175.00
259 ....(with lid) $125.00 - 175.00
260 ....$250.00 - 300.00
261 ....(with lid) $60.00 - 75.00
262 ....$250.00 - 300.00
263 ....(set with lid) $125.00 - 175.00
264 ....$100.00 - 125.00
265 ....$250.00 - 300.00
266 ....$150.00 - 200.00
267 ....(Pot) $275.00 - 325.00
.........................(Cup, each) $40.00 - 50.00
268 ....(Pot) $300.00 - 400.00
...(Cup & Saucer, ea. set) $100.00 - 125.00
269 ....(Pot) $300.00 - 400.00
...(Cup & Saucer, ea. set) $100.00 - 125.00
270 ....(set) $350.00 - 450.00
271 ....(set) $150.00 - 200.00
272 ....$225.00 - 275.00

273 ....$120.00 - 140.00
274 ....$300.00 - 350.00
275 ....$275.00 - 325.00
276 ....$300.00 - 400.00
277 ....$300.00 - 350.00
278 ....$80.00 - 100.00
279 ....$80.00 - 100.00
280 ....$80.00 - 100.00
281 ....$300.00 - 400.00
282 ....$60.00 - 75.00
283 ....$120.00 - 140.00
284 ....$100.00 - 125.00
285 ....$150.00 - 200.00
286 ....$300.00 - 350.00
287 ....$80.00 - 100.00
288 ....$400.00 - 500.00
289 ....(Pot) $400.00 - 500.00
...(Cup & Saucer, ea. set) $100.00 - 125.00
290 ....(Pot) $500.00 - 600.00
...(Cup & Saucer, ea. set) $140.00 - 160.00
291 ....$250.00 - 300.00
292 ....(set) $175.00 - 225.00
293 ....$225.00 - 275.00
294 ....$175.00 - 225.00
295 ....(set) $2000.00 - 2200.00
296 ....$550.00 - 650.00
297 ....$1400.00 - 1600.00
298 ....$1600.00 - 1800.00
299 ....(set) $3000.00 - 4000.00
300 ....$50.00 - 65.00
301 ....$225.00 - 275.00
302 ....$150.00 - 200.00
303 ....$225.00 - 275.00
304 ....$125.00 - 150.00
305 ....(set) $600.00 - 700.00
306 ....$800.00 - 1000.00
307 ....$1200.00 - 1400.00
308 ....$1400.00 - 1600.00
309 ....$1400.00 - 1600.00
310 ....$350.00 - 400.00
311 ....$150.00 - 200.00
312 ....$225.00 - 275.00
313 ....$900.00 - 1100.00
314 ....$350.00 - 400.00
315 ....$325.00 - 375.00
316 ....$325.00 - 375.00
317 ....$175.00 - 225.00
318 ....$3000.00 - 3500.00
319 ....$900.00 - 1100.00
320 ....$3000.00 - 3500.00
321 ....$100.00 - 125.00
322 ....(set) $175.00 - 225.00
323 ....(Pot) $350.00 - 450.00
...(Cup & Saucer, ea. set) $100.00 - 125.00
324 ....(Pot) $350.00 - 450.00
...(Cup & Saucer, ea. set) $100.00 - 125.00
325 ....$70.00 - 90.00
326 ....(set) $225.00 - 275.00

327.....................$400.00 - 500.00
328.....................$350.00 - 400.00
329.................(Pot) $500.00 - 600.00
.....(Cup & Saucer, ea. set) $80.00 - 100.00
330.....................$650.00 - 750.00
331...............$10,000.00 - 12,000.00
332...................$1400.00 - 1600.00
333.....................$350.00 - 400.00
334...................$2500.00 - 3000.00
335.....................$175.00 - 225.00
336.....................$350.00 - 400.00
337.....................$120.00 - 140.00
338.....................$400.00 - 500.00
339.....................$400.00 - 500.00
340.....................$350.00 - 450.00
341.....................$400.00 - 500.00
342.....................$350.00 - 450.00
343.....................$400.00 - 500.00
344.....................$350.00 - 400.00
345.....................$600.00 - 700.00
346...............(set) $250.00 - 300.00
347...............(set) $175.00 - 225.00
348.......................$40.00 - 60.00
349.......................$70.00 - 90.00
350.....................$250.00 - 300.00
351.......................$80.00 - 100.00
352...............(set) $225.00 - 275.00
353...............(set) $225.00 - 275.00
354...............(set) $225.00 - 275.00
355...............(set) $250.00 - 300.00
356...............(set) $250.00 - 300.00
357.....................$120.00 - 140.00
358.............(with lid) $275.00 - 325.00
359.....................$800.00 - 1000.00
360...................$1000.00 - 1200.00
361.....................$275.00 - 325.00
362...................$1400.00 - 1600.00
363.....................$100.00 - 125.00
364............(set) $3500.00 - 4500.00
365.....................$450.00 - 550.00
366.....................$250.00 - 300.00
367.....................$600.00 - 700.00
368...............(set) $250.00 - 300.00
369.....................$700.00 - 800.00
370.....................$450.00 - 550.00
371.....................$500.00 - 600.00
372.....................$600.00 - 700.00
373.....................$700.00 - 800.00
374.....................$150.00 - 175.00
375.....................$300.00 - 350.00
..........(Cream & Sugar) $175.00 - 225.00
.......(Cup & Saucer, ea. set) $70.00 - 80.00
376.....................$150.00 - 175.00
377.....................$150.00 - 175.00
378...............(set) $500.00 - 600.00
379.....................$550.00 - 650.00
380.................(Pot) $600.00 - 700.00

....(Cup & Saucer, ea. set)$100.00 - 125.00
381.....................$325.00 - 375.00
382.....................$200.00 - 250.00
383.....................$250.00 - 300.00
384.....................$325.00 - 375.00
385...............(set) $250.00 - 300.00
386.....................$100.00 - 125.00
387.................(Pot) $500.00 - 600.00
....(Cup & Saucer, ea. set)$100.00 - 125.00
388.......................$60.00 - 70.00
389.......................$75.00 - 100.00
390...............(set) $600.00 - 700.00
391.....................$450.00 - 550.00
392.....................$350.00 - 400.00
393.........(set with lid) $200.00 - 250.00
394.................(Pot) $500.00 - 600.00
.....(Cup & Saucer, ea. set) $80.00 - 100.00
395.....................$175.00 - 225.00
396...................$3000.00 - 3500.00
397.....................$500.00 - 600.00
398...................$2000.00 - 2500.00
399.....................$250.00 - 300.00
400.....................$275.00 - 325.00
401.....................$200.00 - 250.00
402.....................$800.00 - 1000.00
403.....................$500.00 - 600.00
404...................$1400.00 - 1600.00
405...................$1600.00 - 1800.00
406.........................see Plate 405
407.....................$500.00 - 600.00
408.....................$500.00 - 600.00
409.................(Pot) $800.00 - 1000.00
...(Cup & Saucer, ea. set) $150.00 - 275.00
410.................(Pot) $900.00 - 1100.00
...(Cup & Saucer, ea. set) $175.00 - 225.00
411...............(set) $200.00 - 250.00
412.....................$650.00 - 750.00
413...............(set) $200.00 - 250.00
414.....................$500.00 - 600.00
415.....................$175.00 - 225.00
416 (Creamer & Sugar)$200.00 - 250.00
.............(Cup & Saucer) $100.00 - 125.00
417.........(set with lid) $175.00 - 225.00
418.....................$200.00 - 250.00
419.....................$600.00 - 700.00
420.....................$700.00 - 800.00
421.....................$550.00 - 650.00
422...................$1000.00 - 1200.00
423.....................$250.00 - 350.00
424.....................$500.00 - 600.00
425.....................$225.00 - 275.00
426...................$1200.00 - 1400.00
427.....................$550.00 - 650.00
428.....................$600.00 - 700.00
429.....................$900.00 - 1100.00
430.....................$500.00 - 600.00
431.....................$350.00 - 450.00

432.....................$250.00 - 300.00
433.....................$800.00 - 1000.00
434...............(set) $2500.00 - 3000.00
435.....................$100.00 - 125.00
436.....................$250.00 - 300.00
437.....................$175.00 - 225.00
438.....................$325.00 - 375.00
439.....................$3000.00 - 3500.00
440.................(Pot) $650.00 - 750.00
...(Cup & Saucer, ea. set) $100.00 - 125.00
441.....................$3000.00 - 3500.00
442.....................$650.00 - 750.00
443.....................$3000.00 - 3500.00
444.....................$550.00 - 650.00
445.....................$400.00 - 500.00
446...............(set) $5000.00 - 6000.00
447.................(Pot) $3500.00 - 4000.00
...(Cup & Saucer, ea. set) $275.00 - 325.00
448.....................$2800.00 - 3200.00
449 ....See Plate 448
450.....................$250.00 - 300.00
451.....................$550.00 - 650.00
452.....................$600.00 - 700.00
453.....................$550.00 - 650.00
454.....................$275.00 - 325.00
455.....................$275.00 - 325.00
456.....................$300.00 - 350.00
457.....................$250.00 - 300.00
458...............(set) $300.00 - 400.00
459.....................$400.00 - 500.00
460.....................$550.00 - 650.00
461.................(Pot) $500.00 - 600.00
...(Cup & Saucer, ea. set) $100.00 - 125.00
462.....................$350.00 - 450.00
463.....................$350.00 - 400.00
464.....................$120.00 - 140.00
465.....................$100.00 - 125.00
466.....................$100.00 - 125.00
467.....................$120.00 - 140.00
468.....................$450.00 - 550.00
469.....................$3000.00 - 3500.00
470.....................$650.00 - 750.00
471.....................$350.00 - 400.00
472.................(Pot) $2500.00 - 3000.00
..(Creamer and Sugar) $1200.00 - 1400.00
473...............(set) $450.00 - 550.00
474.....................$175.00 - 225.00
475.....................$450.00 - 550.00
476.....................$300.00 - 350.00
477.................(Pot) $550.00 - 650.00
...(Cup & Saucer, ea. set) $100.00 - 125.00
478.....................$350.00 - 400.00
479.....................$375.00 - 425.00
480.....................$350.00 - 400.00
481.....................$275.00 - 325.00
482.....................$550.00 - 650.00
483.......................$70.00 - 90.00

484......................................$300.00 - 350.00
#485......................................$175.00 - 225.00
486..........................(set) $225.00 - 275.00
487..........................(set) $225.00 - 275.00
488......................................$200.00 - 250.00
489......................................$275.00 - 325.00
490......................................$225.00 - 275.00
491......................................$200.00 - 250.00
492......................................$225.00 - 275.00
493......................................$175.00 - 225.00
494......................................$150.00 - 200.00
495......................................$250.00 - 300.00
496......................................$175.00 - 225.00
497......................................$175.00 - 225.00
498......................................$200.00 - 250.00
499......................................$175.00 - 225.00
500......................................$175.00 - 225.00
501......................................$150.00 - 200.00
502......................................$200.00 - 250.00
503......................................$150.00 - 200.00
504......................................$200.00 - 250.00
505......................................$200.00 - 250.00
506..........................(Box) $225.00 - 275.00
..............(Hair Receiver) $200.00 - 250.00
507......................................$300.00 - 400.00
508......................................$175.00 - 225.00
509......................................$100.00 - 125.00
510......................................$225.00 - 275.00
511......................................$225.00 - 275.00
512......................................$225.00 - 275.00
513......................................$225.00 - 275.00
514......................................$175.00 - 200.00
515......................................$200.00 - 225.00
516......................................$200.00 - 225.00
517......................................$300.00 - 400.00
518......................................$300.00 - 350.00
519......................................$350.00 - 450.00
520......................................$500.00 - 600.00

521......................................$300.00 - 350.00
522......................................$225.00 - 275.00
523......................................$1600.00 - 1800.00
524......................................$500.00 - 600.00
525......................................$1600.00 - 1800.00
526......................................$600.00 - 800.00
527..................(pair) $4000.00 - 4500.00
528..See Plate 527
529......................................$500.00 - 600.00
530..See Plate 529
531......................................$1000.00 - 1200.00
532......................................$250.00 - 300.00
533......................................$600.00 - 800.00
534......................................$600.00 - 700.00
535......................................$300.00 - 400.00
536......................................$600.00 - 800.00
537......................................$500.00 - 600.00
538......................(pair) $500.00 - 600.00
539......................................$300.00 - 400.00
540......................................$800.00 - 1000.00
541......................................$600.00 - 700.00
542......................$8000.00 - 10,000.00
543......................................$3000.00 - 4000.00
544......................................$400.00 - 500.00
545......................................$2500.00 - 2800.00
546......................................$400.00 - 500.00
547......................................$3000.00 - 4000.00
548......................................$350.00 - 450.00
549......................$10,000.00 - 12,000.00
550......................................$500.00 - 600.00
551......................................$500.00 - 600.00
552......................................$600.00 - 800.00
553..See Plate 552
554......................................$2500.00 - 2800.00
555......................................$500.00 - 600.00
556......................................$1000.00 - 1200.00
557......................................$500.00 - 600.00
558......................................$500.00 - 600.00

559......................................$1000.00 - 1200.00
560......................................$1400.00 - 1600.00
561......................................$1000.00 - 1200.00
562......................................$1400.00 - 1600.00
563......................(ea.) $300.00 - 400.00
564......................................$450.00 - 550.00
565......................................$3000.00 - 3500.00
566......................................$800.00 - 1000.00
567......................................$3500.00 - 3800.00
568......................................$1800.00 - 2000.00
569......................................$1600.00 - 1800.00
570......................................$500.00 - 600.00
571......................................$1200.00 - 1400.00
572......................................$1000.00 - 1200.00
573......................................$225.00 - 275.00
574......................................$1800.00 - 2000.00
575......................................$600.00 - 700.00
576......................................$1000.00 - 1200.00
577..See Plate 576
578......................................$1200.00 - 1400.00
579......................................$1000.00 - 1200.00
580......................................$800.00 - 1000.00
581......................................$1800.00 - 2000.00
582......................................$2500.00 - 3000.00
583......................................$3000.00 - 3500.00
584......................................$40.00 - 50.00
585..............(with lid) $100.00 - 125.00
586......................................$30.00 - 40.00
587......................................$200.00 - 250.00
588......................................$125.00 - 150.00
589......................................$125.00 - 150.00
590......................................$125.00 - 150.00
591......................................$40.00 - 50.00
592......................................$225.00 - 275.00
593......................................$150.00 - 175.00
594......................................$500.00 - 600.00
595......................................$550.00 - 650.00

Books on Antiques and Collectibles

This is only a partial listing of the books on antiques that are available from Collector Books. All books are well illustrated and contain current values. Most of the following books are available from your local book seller, antique dealer, or public library. If you are unable to locate certain titles in your area, you may order by mail from COLLECTOR BOOKS, P.O. Box 3009, Paducah, KY 42002-3009. Customers with Visa or MasterCard may phone in orders from 8:00 – 4:00 CST, M – F – Toll Free 1-800-626-5420. Add $2.00 for postage for the first book ordered and $0.30 for each additional book. Include item number, title, and price when ordering. Allow 14 to 21 days for delivery.

BOOKS ON GLASS AND POTTERY

1810	American Art Glass, Shuman	$29.95
2016	Bedroom & Bathroom Glassware of the Depression Years	$19.95
1312	Blue & White Stoneware, McNerney	$9.95
1959	Blue Willow, 2nd Ed., Gaston	$14.95
3719	Coll. Glassware from the 40's, 50's, 60's, 2nd Ed., Florence	$19.95
3311	Collecting Yellow Ware – Id. & Value Gd., McAllister	$16.95
2352	Collector's Ency. of Akro Agate Glassware, Florence	$14.95
1373	Collector's Ency. of American Dinnerware, Cunningham	24.95
2272	Collector's Ency. of California Pottery, Chipman	$24.95
3312	Collector's Ency. of Children's Dishes, Whitmyer	$19.95
2133	Collector's Ency. of Cookie Jars, Roerig	$24.95
3724	Collector's Ency. of Depression Glass, 11th Ed., Florence	$19.95
2209	Collector's Ency. of Fiesta, 7th Ed., Huxford	$19.95
1439	Collector's Ency. of Flow Blue China, Gaston	$19.95
1915	Collector's Ency. of Hall China, 2nd Ed., Whitmyer	$19.95
2334	Collector's Ency. of Majolica Pottery, Katz-Marks	$19.95
1358	Collector's Ency. of McCoy Pottery, Huxford	$19.95
3313	Collector's Ency. of Niloak, Gifford	$19.95
1039	Collector's Ency. of Nippon Porcelain I, Van Patten	$19.95
2089	Collector's Ency. of Nippon Porcelain II, Van Patten	$24.95
1665	Collector's Ency. of Nippon Porcelain III, Van Patten	$24.95
1447	Collector's Ency. of Noritake, 1st Series, Van Patten	$19.95
1034	Collector's Ency. of Roseville Pottery, Huxford	$19.95
1035	Collector's Ency. of Roseville Pottery, 2nd Ed., Huxford	$19.95
3314	Collector's Ency. of Van Briggle Art Pottery, Sasicki	$24.95
3433	Collector's Guide To Harker Pottery -U.S.A., Colbert	$17.95
2339	Collector's Guide to Shawnee Pottery, Vanderbilt	$19.95
1425	Cookie Jars, Westfall	$9.95
3440	Cookie Jars, Book II, Westfall	$19.95
2275	Czechoslovakian Glass & Collectibles, Barta	$16.95
3315	Elegant Glassware of the Depression Era, 5th Ed., Florence	$19.95
3318	Glass Animals of the Depression Era, Garmon & Spencer	$19.95
2024	Kitchen Glassware of the Depression Years, 4th Ed., Florence	$19.95
3322	Pocket Guide to Depression Glass, 8th Ed., Florence	$9.95
1670	Red Wing Collectibles, DePasquale	$9.95
1440	Red Wing Stoneware, DePasquale	$9.95
1958	So. Potteries Blue Ridge Dinnerware, 3rd Ed., Newbound	$14.95
3739	Standard Carnival Glass, 4th Ed., Edwards	$24.95
1848	Very Rare Glassware of the Depression Years, Florence	$24.95
2140	Very Rare Glassware of the Depression Years, Second Series	$24.95
3326	Very Rare Glassware of the Depression Years, Third Series	$24.95
3327	Watt Pottery – Identification & Value Guide, Morris	$19.95
2224	World of Salt Shakers, 2nd Ed., Lechner	$24.95

BOOKS ON DOLLS & TOYS

2079	Barbie Fashion, Vol. 1, 1959-1967, Eames	$24.95
3310	Black Dolls – 1820 - 1991 – Id. & Value Guide, Perkins	$17.95
1514	Character Toys & Collectibles, 1st Series, Longest	$19.95
1750	Character Toys & Collectibles, 2nd Series, Longest	$19.95
1529	Collector's Ency. of Barbie Dolls, DeWein	$19.95
2338	Collector's Ency. of Disneyana, Longest & Stern	$24.95
3441	Madame Alexander Price Guide #18, Smith	$9.95
1540	Modern Toys, 1930 - 1980, Baker	$19.95
3442	Patricia Smith's Doll Values – Antique to Modern, 9th ed.	$12.95
1886	Stern's Guide to Disney	$14.95

2139	Stern's Guide to Disney, 2nd Series	$14.95
1513	Teddy Bears & Steiff Animals, Mandel	$9.95
1817	Teddy Bears & Steiff Animals, 2nd Series, Mandel	$19.95
2084	Teddy Bears, Annalees & Steiff Animals, 3rd Series, Mandel	$19.95
2028	Toys, Antique & Collectible, Longest	$14.95
1808	Wonder of Barbie, Manos	$9.95
1430	World of Barbie Dolls, Manos	$9.95

OTHER COLLECTIBLES

1457	American Oak Furniture, McNerney	$9.95
2269	Antique Brass & Copper, Gaston	$16.95
2333	Antique & Collectible Marbles, 3rd Ed., Grist	$9.95
1712	Antique & Collectible Thimbles, Mathis	$19.95
1748	Antique Purses, Holiner	$19.95
1868	Antique Tools, Our American Heritage, McNerney	$9.95
1426	Arrowheads & Projectile Points, Hothem	$7.95
1278	Art Nouveau & Art Deco Jewelry, Baker	$9.95
1714	Black Collectibles, Gibbs	$19.95
1128	Bottle Pricing Guide, 3rd Ed., Cleveland	$7.95
1752	Christmas Ornaments, Johnston	$19.95
2132	Collector's Ency. of American Furniture, Vol. I, Swedberg	$24.95
2271	Collector's Ency. of American Furniture, Vol. II, Swedberg	$24.95
2018	Collector's Ency. of Granite Ware, Greguire	$24.95
3430	Coll. Ency. of Granite Ware, Book 2, Greguire	$24.95
2083	Collector's Ency. of Russel Wright Designs, Kerr	$19.95
2337	Collector's Guide to Decoys, Book II, Huxford	$16.95
2340	Collector's Guide to Easter Collectibles, Burnett	$16.95
1441	Collector's Guide to Post Cards, Wood	$9.95
2276	Decoys, Kangas	$24.95
1629	Doorstops – Id. & Values, Bertoia	$9.95
1716	Fifty Years of Fashion Jewelry, Baker	$19.95
3316	Flea Market Trader, 8th Ed., Huxford	$9.95
3317	Florence's Standard Baseball Card Price Gd., 5th Ed.	$9.95
1755	Furniture of the Depression Era, Swedberg	$19.95
3436	Grist's Big Book of Marbles, Everett Grist	$19.95
2278	Grist's Machine Made & Contemporary Marbles	$9.95
1424	Hatpins & Hatpin Holders, Baker	$9.95
3319	Huxford's Collectible Advertising – Id. & Value Gd.	$17.95
3439	Huxford's Old Book Value Guide, 5th Ed.	$19.95
1181	100 Years of Collectible Jewelry, Baker	$9.95
2023	Keen Kutter Collectibles, 2nd Ed., Heuring	$14.95
2216	Kitchen Antiques – 1790 - 1940, McNerney	$14.95
3320	Modern Guns – Id. & Val. Gd., 9th Ed., Quertermous	$12.95
1965	Pine Furniture, Our American Heritage, McNerney	$14.95
3321	Ornamental & Figural Nutcrackers, Rittenhouse	$16.95
2026	Railroad Collectibles, 4th Ed., Baker	$14.95
1632	Salt & Pepper Shakers, Guarnaccia	$9.95
1888	Salt & Pepper Shakers II, Guarnaccia	$14.95
2220	Salt & Pepper Shakers III, Guarnaccia	$14.95
3443	Salt & Pepper Shakers IV, Guarnaccia	$18.95
3737	Schroeder's Antiques Price Guide, 12th Ed.	$12.95
2096	Silverplated Flatware, 4th Ed., Hagan	$14.95
3325	Standard Knife Collector's Guide, 2nd Ed., Stewart	$12.95
2348	20th Century Fashionable Plastic Jewelry, Baker	$19.95
3444	Wanted To Buy, 4th Ed.	$9.95

Schroeder's ANTIQUES Price Guide

. . . is the #1 best-selling antiques & collectibles value guide on the market today, and here's why . . .

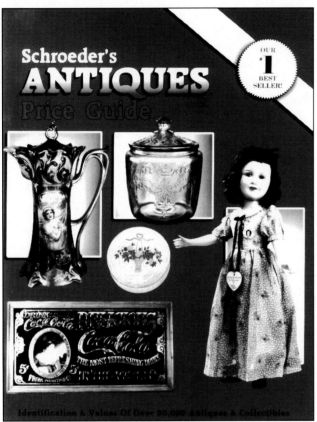

8½ x 11, 608 Pages, $12.95

• More than 300 advisors, well-known dealers, and top-notch collectors work together with our editors to bring you accurate information regarding pricing and identification.

• More than 45,000 items in almost 500 categories are listed along with hundreds of sharp original photos that illustrate not only the rare and unusual, but the common, popular collectibles as well.

• Each large close-up shot shows important details clearly. Every subject is represented with histories and background information, a feature not found in any of our competitors' publications.

• Our editors keep abreast of newly-developing trends, often adding several new categories a year as the need arises.

If it merits the interest of today's collector, you'll find it in *Schroeder's*. And you can feel confident that the information we publish is up to date and accurate. Our advisors thoroughly check each category to spot inconsistencies, listings that may not be entirely reflective of market dealings, and lines too vague to be of merit. Only the best of the lot remains for publication.

Without doubt, you'll find
SCHROEDER'S ANTIQUES PRICE GUIDE
the only one to buy for
reliable information and values.

COLLECTOR BOOKS
A Division of Schroeder Publishing Co., Inc.